THE
GENESIS
PRINCIPLE

THE GENESIS PRINCIPLE

The ABC's of Throwing Disorganization,
Procrastination and Personal Humiliation
Out of Your Life Forever

Patty Chirico

DEDICATION

I dedicate this book to my wonderful Mom, Christine Chirico Lorenzen, and to the loving memory of my Dad, Philip Michael Chirico. They are the ones who taught me many principles of life, including a commitment to excellence.

My precious Mom has upheld me daily in prayer. Her faithfulness to pray for me has meant more to me than anything else she could have done. This book has been a labor of love, and she has stood with me, always encouraging, supporting, and helping me give birth to the vision God planted in my heart. Mom, I am forever thankful to God for you and for the many wonderful years we had with Daddy.

Until the day Daddy died of cancer in 1986, he encouraged me, "Always seek to find a better way to do something." That thought has been a driving force behind the success of my organizing according to Biblical principles.

ACKNOWLEDGMENTS

My deepest gratitude goes to my beloved sister, Terri Chirico Strong, who first caught the vision of me becoming a Professional Organizer. In those difficult early years, before I ever understood organizing or even heard the title, "Professional Organizer," Terri encouraged me to keep going. She told me that there was something more to my calling than I could understand at the time. She said, "Don't give up." She stood with me, constantly encouraging and promoting me through the years. Terri gave clarity and purpose to my vision. She is the one who set me on the right course. For her, I am eternally thankful to God.

Many other people—family, friends, and strangers—for years have encouraged me to write a book on the Biblical principles of organizing. Chris Strong, my brother-in-law, often confirmed my thoughts and gave new insights into the Scriptural understanding of organizing. Ted Lorenzen, my step-father, was always there, ready to help whenever I needed him. Beth and Mark

Lane gave tireless hours of proofing, editing, feedback, insight, ideas, and patience with me.

Many people were in constant prayer for me and this book, especially my faithful church family at The Church of Jesus Our Shepherd; the prayer warriors of Partners in Ministry; Deborah Abercrombie, Judy Brassfield, Renee Strickland, Lisa Bell, and Debbie Chambers in my home bible study group; and the many wonderful ladies in my BSF (Bible Study Fellowship).

Sandra Felton encouraged me to write this book and take it to other countries. Donald Bloom caught my vision to help millions of people around the world to get organized. Pat Springle of Baxter Press kept my feet to the fire with great encouragement and direction. And finally, Tom Williford came into my life during those final months when I was struggling to complete the book and supported me with great love and care. He helped me believe in myself enough to finish it. I thank God for surrounding me with such strong support.

My deep thanks and appreciation to each and everyone of you!

CONTENTS

INTRODUCTION

GP

This book uncovers the very first ancient blueprints of order and gives you the tools you need to throw disorganization, procrastination, and the resulting humiliation out of your life forever.

The concepts outlined in these pages provide the tools to effectively and decisively deal with these issues for the rest of your life. Please don't misunderstand: It doesn't mean you will get organized and automatically stay that way, and it doesn't mean you will magically conquer procrastination and never put things off again. But now you have the effective decision-making tools that apply in *all* areas of your life *all* the time. Forever. You don't have to look for some hidden secret anymore.

You will learn to create order in your life by building a solid foundation of simplicity and strength, much like building a house. A strong foundation of order works in every environment: in closets, kitchens, basements, garages, and purses; on planes, trains, and automobiles; in attics and with antiques; in workrooms, storerooms, and playrooms; in large corporate offices and small home offices; for doctors, dentists, and dieticians; and in barns, bathrooms, and briefcases.

When you finish building a house and move in, the work still continues. In fact, the work has just begun. If the house is built of wood, it will need repainting at some point. New types of paints, colors, and methods will be developed, but the original structure of the house remains intact. And in a dozen ways, a house requires continual maintenance. You have to clean and vacuum, replace filters, and of course, pay the bills. Even a perfectly landscaped lawn needs constant care. If the house is built with a very strong foundation, it will easily last your entire lifetime—but the maintenance never stops.

The Biblical principles in this book are a foundation for order in your life. They are the practical applications of God's Word: simple, time-tested, and proven. They will not tell you exactly where to put the clothes in your closet or the tools in the garage, but these organizing principles provide skills for making decisions in organizing every area of your life and keeping order forever.

This book is for both the disorganized and the organized—from those who *feel* order is impossible to those who are so organized they have *never understood* the concept of impossible, from those who fail often to those who are driven to avoid failure at all costs.

If you have struggled with disorder and have never known where to start, this book will give you solid handles. For those who start over and over again but never finish, you will learn how to make progress and stay organized. If you are naturally organized, this book will help you increase, define, and refine your organization skills. It will put a name to some of the things you are already successfully doing (but perhaps never knew you were doing them right). If you are a compulsive organizer, these principles will help you relax and enjoy your strengths of discipline and order.

You will discover that this book is excellent for the coffee table and for bathroom reading when you only have a few minutes to look at a page or two. The content builds and the chapters flow from one to the next, but each chapter is easily understood on its own and stands alone. To acquire the most benefit, I recommend that you first read this book from cover to cover. Then go back and reference specific chapters which are applicable to your particular situation when you need help.

If your mind feels cluttered—if you find it difficult to sit down and finish a book, or have good intentions but never really get started, or when you do get started, you lose it somewhere—this book will help you. Though everyone can be helped by this book, it is written primarily for those of us who have a cluttered mind.

If you have a Bible, open it and read along in the references. If you don't own a copy, now is the time to purchase one. Many good translations are available. Find one you personally enjoy and feel comfortable using.

God's Word has every answer for us, including how to organize our lives, throw away seemingly valuable junk, and clean out those messy closets. Enjoy and have fun as you organize your life!

Chapter 1
TRUE STORIES

GP

God has made each of us incredibly gifted and unique individuals. Some of those gifts are prominent in our left brains where we do things in an orderly way, take notes in a straight line, and balance checkbooks to the very last penny. Some of us are right-brained and creative. We write all over a page, draw diagrams and symbols, and use splashes of color with pens, pencils, and highlighters. We have difficulty making ourselves balance our checkbooks at all. If we just come close, we are thrilled.

I am one of those right-brained people. *Very* right-brained. As I sit here and write a book about organizing, my own checkbook needs balancing. My mind just has a hard time focusing and thinking logically about little details such as columns of numbers. I would rather get up in front of a thousand people on the spur of the moment and give a speech. That doesn't mean anything to my bankers who, thank God, have been patient and understanding with me. I live in the small city of Gainesville,

Georgia, and my reputation of being "the organizer" can sometimes have its drawbacks. Everywhere I go, people expect me to *always* have everything in perfect order. I won't and never will, but now I usually can find anything I need in thirty seconds—except the mistake hidden somewhere in my checkbook. I am thankful for the many wonderful people with a delightful sense of humor who help me with my own struggles. I tell my own stories in the next chapter.

Scores of people have asked me to help them become more organized. They have said these things to me:

— "I have a very hard time letting go. I keep everything."

— "I buy books on organizing, but I lose them somewhere."

— "I've tried to get organized before, but it never stays that way."

— "My clutter is like a wall. It feels comfortable to me and insulates me from others."

— "I know I have a lot of junk, but where do I start?"

— "I would be too embarrassed for anyone to see my mess."

— "When I look at all this mess, I feel completely defeated. That's why I don't even start."

— "I never can find anything. I lose everything."

— "I never have time to have fun because I feel like I should always be cleaning up my mess."

— "My husband is such a pack-rat. He even picks things out of the trash on curbs. He brings them home, never uses them for two years, so I eventually throw them away.

Then he picks them out of our own trash, telling me, 'But I can use that!' "

— "I never catch up. The harder I work, the more behind I am."

— "My wife is home all day and our house is always a mess."

— "I feel like crying when I look at my mess."

— "I will be your first failure. I'm the only one I know who can't get organized."

— "I'm always afraid that someone is going to drop in and see my messy house."

— "I know my outer clutter has something to do with inner clutter. I just don't know what to do about it."

— "I'm so afraid something will happen to me and people will see what a mess I am."

— "I can't have guests because I can't find the guest bed."

— "Just looking at my mess makes me tired and exhausted."

— "Can't we just set a match to it all and burn it?"

— "My car is a mess. I'm embarrassed when someone unexpectedly rides with me."

— "I ran out of room in my house, so I have a box of junk riding around in my van."

— "I don't even want to go home because my house is so messy."

— "My purse is like a suitcase. It has everything in it, but I have a hard time finding anything."

— "I'm always buying new things/ tools/ clothes because I can't find the ones I already have."

— "I'm a perfectionist, but my spouse is really messy."

— "If I don't get organized, I think my spouse will leave me."

— "I know I have one of those, but where did I put it?"

— "I'll get organized . . . when I get time."

— "I love order, but my family won't cooperate."

— "In this house, we never throw anything away."

— "This room looks bad, but you should see my attic. No, on second thought, I'm not letting you see my attic. You'll get too scared and think we really are impossible."

— "We were very organized before we had children."

— "We're always late because we can't find belts, shoes, keys, or . . . ."

— "I'm organized at my office, so why am I such a mess at home?"

— "I'm organized in my home, so why am I such a mess at the office?"

— "Before I retired, my office was always neat as a pin. Of course, I had a full-time secretary then. Do you think that makes the difference?"

— "The only thing we ever fight about is the mess in our house. I blame her and she blames me."

— "We are supposed to be sharing a closet, but my wife takes up 90% of the space. She has several hundred pairs of shoes. Shoes are everywhere! I should buy stock in the shoe stores."

— "He has hats all over the house. Everywhere I look— hats, hats, and more hats. I'm so sick of these hats everywhere."

— "My husband throws his clothes all over the place. Why can't he just simply hang them up?"

— "Don't look under the bed. There's probably something growing under there."

My prayer is that this book will help you to be honest with yourself, appreciate your strengths and weaknesses, and enable you to one day tell your own story. This book includes many personal stories to give you real-life examples and inspiration in your own quest to organize your life. All of the stories are true. Each and every person graciously gave me permission to use their own experience in bringing order to their lives. In some of the very personal stories, the names, geographical locations, and identifying circumstances were changed to protect their privacy. In other cases, they told me to "let it all hang out."

The organizing work that I do with my clients is highly confidential, as it is with all Professional Organizers who adhere to our code of ethics as members of The National Association of Professional Organizers (NAPO). Our work is similar to that of a doctor, lawyer, or CPA who values his clients, their needs, and their privacy.

I am forever thankful to all of those brave people who allowed me into the areas of their lives where no one had tread before. I have seen it all: the good, the bad, and the ugly, and I appreciate the courage and commitment of these people to grasp and apply the principles of change.

Chapter 2
A FORMER CLUTTERED MESS

GP

Yes, it's true. I was a former cluttered mess, and this is my story. I have some areas of my life that I am still working on. Getting my life in order requires change—constant change. It's a process that will not be complete until I die and arrive on time in the presence of God. I hope you'll be there, too. It is the only place without clutter or clocks, and where disorder, procrastination, and humiliation do not exist.

In all of my travels, people always ask me the same question, "How did you become a Professional Organizer?" I've come a long way. I was a mess. In fact, I used to be one of those "messies" as Sandra Felton, author of *The Messies Manual,* so aptly describes people like me. If I had one of her wonderful books years ago, it probably would have gotten buried in the bottom of a closet just like the other books on organizing I used to buy. Never read any of them. Never could even find them after I brought them home.

But no more! The fact is, some of you reading this book are naturally more organized than me, but I have learned the skill of implementing Biblical principles in every area of my life, particularly in the problem of disorganization. Now I can almost always *find anything I need in thirty seconds.* What a wonderful feeling!

Eleven years ago, I couldn't say that. When I was a mess, I was the only one who knew the truth—the only one, that is, except God, my family, and close friends. They saw my problem very clearly, but they all loved me anyway. *Especially* God. Deep within, I was humiliated and I didn't love myself very much, but no one knew that. *Except* God. I put on a good front. On the outside, I looked like everything was fine. Deep inside, things were a mess. My home was an outer reflection of the inner me. My clutter was hidden. When friends came over, my house usually looked very neat and clean. Of course, I never wanted anyone to just pop in on the spur of the moment.

"I'm a very private person," I would say. "Always call me first." The truth is, I needed time to throw things in drawers, under the bed, and into the closets before they arrived. My beloved childhood friend, Judy Brassfield, reminded me of something funny recently during one of my seminars. We laughed (and so did everyone else in the seminar) about the times when company suddenly came over. I grabbed all the things sitting on the kitchen counter and hid them in the oven! To see me now, no one could believe it, but it was true. Judy is one of those people who loved me in spite of my craziness, and she still does after all these years.

I had a storage room the size of a garage, which cost me a significant amount of money, and yet it was full of junk—*full*—from front to back and top to floor. My junk was costing me a monthly fee! The clutter in my heart was just the same, hidden in darkness, just like the clutter hiding behind the oven door and the junk lurking behind the storage room door. And I paid a high price there, too. My heart's clutter cost me inner peace. Everyone but me seemed to think I had my life "together" because I put on a good front, but I lived in fear that one day I would wake up and the world would know that I was a mess, inside and out.

I ran to hide from the humiliation which was hiding in my heart. I ran to work where I spent many long, hard hours. I determined to stay too busy to face the truth. I would never have admitted it then, but my career was number one on my priority list. My life was totally out of balance, and my priorities were a mess. Then, one night something very dramatic and life-changing happened to me.

On a Saturday night in the early spring of 1989, I was sitting at a large round table in a formal ballroom, attending a convention as a representative for my company. The event was a necessary part of the social networking for my career in sales. Although I came alone, I was surrounded by friends and colleagues and was having a delightful time. I loved my job, especially the socializing part of it. (It was the paperwork that always got to me.)

At that moment, I was sitting quietly when all of a sudden, I seemed to be pulled up inside a clear bubble high above the crowd of hundreds of people. I was looking down at everyone partying, and I looked at myself. At that moment, God gave me insight. I thought, "What am I doing here? I'm just playing a lot of meaningless games with my life like so many of these other people." It was as though the scales came off my eyes, and I saw how meaningless my life had become. I said, "I don't want to do this anymore." Then, just as suddenly, I was back in my seat. Again, I looked all around and saw the same thing. I knew that something monumental had just changed inside of me. I immediately got up, retrieved my coat, and left for home.

I realized that I had been playing games with God. Although I went to church every Sunday and had known Him as my Lord and Savior for many years, my heart was with Him only on Sundays. The rest of the week, I was too busy to think about God. Now, I had a deep hunger to *embrace* Him in every area of my life.

The following Monday morning, I walked from my car into my office. I looked up into the beautiful blue sky, then I looked at my hands and prayed a prayer: "Lord, there must be something different I can do with these hands. I don't want to play these games anymore!"

We have a God who answers prayer, so we must remember the importance of how we pray. Two weeks later,

I lost my job. I was devastated. A friend recommended that I should try fasting and prayer, and since I was desperate, I was ready to try anything. Previously, I thought fasting was only for "those other people." Funny how it sometimes takes a crisis to stop us long enough to truly get us on our faces before God. . . .

The one day I scheduled for fasting and prayer turned into a three-month period of time of almost constant prayer and various forms of fasting. I don't mean to say that I didn't eat for three months, but most days I gave up something—one or more meals, or part of a meal, or something special I wanted. The important thing is not how much food I gave up, but how much time I spent with God and in His Word. In place of the physical eating, I literally feasted on His Word, the Bread of Life, and my own life was transformed as a result. People all around me saw a dramatic change for the better. When I ran into someone while out on errands, they commented about how my face glowed and how much younger and peaceful I looked. I found the presence of God to be wonderfully rejuvenating and life-giving!

During that three-month period of time, I also began to face my clutter for the first time in my life. I started first by cleaning out the internal clutter—those areas within me that harbored unforgiveness, anger, bitterness, pain, and shame. I noticed that when I allowed the Lord to shed His light on the hidden closets deep within me that I suddenly would see my external clutter with new eyes. I was amazed at the new ability and strength to purge the outside clutter. The more I purged on the outside—my bedroom closet, my storage room, my home office—the easier it became to deal with the internal clutter. The more internal clutter I cleaned, the more I understood how to get rid of the external clutter. And so it was—a cleaning inside and out.

I began to see that my *external clutter* is directly related to *internal clutter*. My home, my heart, and my soul began to reflect the newly organized me. I was learning to *embrace God* in every aspect of my life.

As people noticed this transformation, they started asking me to help them organize their lives. What a shock! I was stunned to think anyone would want my help, but each person was desperate. I said, "Yes," but then I had to frantically figure out how to help them. I looked to God's Word and began to see Biblical principles of organization. He is a God of order, and everything He created is in perfect order; we are the ones who have made a mess of things. I learned that by emulating Him in the steps of creation, we can create order in our lives.

When I began to implement these Biblical principles with other people, they always worked—much to my surprise at the time! Since 1989, they are still working with hundreds of clients. These are the principles I am sharing in this book. I have been teaching them in seminars across the United States and in Europe. They have worked for everyone willing to follow them, and they will work for you. If my greatest weakness could be turned into a strength to help others, the same can happen in your life. No matter how messy you are, you can get organized if you are willing to change and learn a few new skills.

The first important principle I learned in getting organized is The 3-E's Principle.

The 3-E's Principle

A. Especially God

Some people will love you the way you are, but *especially* God. He will always love you, clutter and all.

B. Except God

You can hide everything from everyone *except* God. He knows it all; nothing is hidden, and He still loves you.

C. Embrace God

He cares about every detail of your life and wants to help you in organizing. He is a gentlemen and will not force Himself into your life. Just ask Him for help, *embrace* and trust Him.

Chapter 3
FIND ANYTHING IN THIRTY SECONDS

GP

I don't know if Noah Webster's desk and closets were organized, but his books were very organized. He was an exceptionally busy man. He graduated from Yale and was a schoolmaster, lawyer, journalist, and legislator. He founded a magazine and two newspapers in New York and was a leader in the founding of Amherst College.

Born in 1758, Noah Webster is famous for publishing a spelling book in 1783 and his first dictionary in 1806, which contained about 40,000 words with brief definitions. He spent years in language study and research to prepare for his masterpiece, *An American Dictionary of the English Language*, published in 1828. This edition contained about 70,000 entries. Today, *Webster's Dictionary* is the most widely respected dictionary in our language.

Among the hundreds of books in Webster's personal library, he said he could find any book he needed in thirty seconds. I have not been able to discover his method of organization, but I have read about his deep faith in God and his belief in God's Word. I have often wondered if the Biblical principles I use with my clients are the same ones Noah Webster used in organizing his books and his dictionary. He continually worked on improving his dictionary with new editions throughout the years. We can learn a lot of lessons from his life.

Our first goal is to understand what it means to be organized.

> Being organized is the ability to find anything you need in thirty seconds.

Being organized does not imply perfection, nor does it mean that everything will always be clean. It means that when you are trying to find something, you know exactly where to look. If you leave your home or office, you can call a perfect stranger and direct him how to find a particular item. That is the real test of order. I can tell you that when you get to that point, it is the greatest feeling!

One of my great joys now is to have company and know that my house, while it may not always be perfectly clean, it is usually in order and ready for friends to drop in. When I have company and they are looking for something, it's usually easy to find. My niece Jennifer and nephew Nick visit me and playfully challenge my organizational skills. When they need to find something, they try to see if I can help them find it in thirty seconds.

I then instruct them precisely which closet, shelf, or drawer to look for it. Remember my story—I am the one who used to hide things in the oven! Set your first goal of finding anything you need in thirty seconds, but be realistic. It won't happen overnight. It took Noah Webster twenty-two years to add 30,000 more entries to his dictionary, nearly doubling the size of his first edition. He was busy, but diligent and focused on adding more details to his masterpiece. We will talk about the details of getting organized in later chapters. While it won't take you twenty-two years to get organized, it *is* a process which you can continually improve and fine-tune. Not everything will be in it's place *all* the time—just *most* of the time. When you are reading the paper, it may be spread out on the coffee table during those leisure hours. However, when you are through with it, the paper should have a particular place to go. The idea is that when you start to put it up, you know exactly where to put it.

Don't be too detailed at first. Think of your organizing project as *your* masterpiece. When you are through, it will feel like a great accomplishment.

The next time you look up a word in the dictionary or use spell check on your computer, think about Noah Webster and his ability to find any book in thirty seconds. If you apply the principles in this book, you will be able to find anything in thirty seconds, too!

WHAT DOES IT MEAN TO BE ORGANIZED?

Being organized
is the ability
to find anything you need
in
thirty seconds.

Chapter 4
THE GENESIS PRINCIPLE

GP

In the beginning God created the heavens and the earth. (Genesis 1:1)

The first chapter of the first book of the Bible describes The Genesis Principle of four steps of organization. In His creation, God is the author of both creativity and order. Look around at the incredible color, diversity—and humor—in God's creation. Pelicans, giraffes, oak trees, jonquils, and constellations of stars are a part of the fabulous diversity God made. And yet in all its diversity, it all fits together in harmony and order.

Some of us are very creative, but we struggle with disorder. We love to make something fresh and new, but we never seem to finish or never seem to get cleaned up. And some of us never seem to get beyond our great ideas to get started.

Others of us are so ordered, it's painful! We rigidly and dogmatically put everything in its place, and we can't stand anything new and creative because it messes up our regimented lives.

And quite often, these people live together!

God is not "either/or" when it comes to creativity and order. He's "both/and." He blends His artistic flair with His commitment to have things work smoothly enough. And at each step of creation, He said, "It is good."

I believe the imbalance that many of us experience, either creativity without order or order without creativity, is caused by fear. In his letter to Timothy, the apostle Paul wrote, "For God did not give us a spirit of timidity, but a spirit of power, of love and of self-discipline" (II Timothy 1:7). What are messy and rigid people afraid of? They may be afraid that:

—if they even try to be creative, they will fail.

—if they try to be ordered, but fail, there's no use to try again.

—others will criticize them or make fun of them if they try to change.

—they may not have the courage to follow through with their commitment to change, so it's better not to start.

—if they fail one more time, they will be overwhelmed with feelings of shame.

Each of us has God-given strengths, and each of these strengths has corresponding weaknesses. Our goal is to live primarily in our strengths without letting our weaknesses (or others' criticism of them) dominate us. A free-spirited, creative person doesn't need to become rigidly ordered, just ordered enough to let his creativity soar unimpeded. And a naturally ordered person doesn't need to become completely uninhibited. But he will be much more fulfilled if he finds an outlet for his long-repressed, God-given creativity.

Begin the process of reordering your thinking about organization by recognizing the fact that God is the author of both creativity and order. Both. Not one or the other. And He will give us the wisdom and strength to find the balance of these two characteristics in our lives if we trust Him to lead us. Why don't you ask Him now?

The Genesis Principle is a four step process which unlocks the secret of creativity and order found in God's design of creation. Each of us can follow this plan and find peace, simplicity, and freedom.

Most of my clients make a big mistake when they start to organize: They first find a place for everything they intend to keep. Certainly, that is a very important step—the *last* step. If we start by finding places for things, we end up just "rearranging our overabundance," as Hamid, a gentleman attending one of my seminars accurately observed. We are not going to be successful in getting organized unless we follow a plan. A good plan is easy to implement if it has a system of steps that flow and make good sense.

The best plan I have seen is God's plan of creation. If we look at the steps God took while creating the world and everything in it, we will learn a lot. His plan is quite sensible and easy to follow. It flows.

These steps give you the insights and skills you need to organize every area of your life. Since 1989, I have gone into hundreds of seemingly impossible situations in all kinds of settings, both home and professional, and brought order by utilizing these basic steps. They are the keys to organizing every area, no matter how messy, overwhelming, or seemingly impossible you think your situation may be. These four steps are your foundation to begin your own creation of order in every area of your life:

1. Separate
2. Combine
3. Evaluate
4. Assign

The opening chapters of the Bible describe how God instituted this plan step-by-step in the created order of the universe. We will examine each of these steps in detail in the following chapters.

One of the secrets to getting organized and staying organized is: *the steps must be accomplished in order.* Learn them well, say them out loud, and memorize them in sequence.

Chapter 5
STEP ONE: SEPARATE

GP

1. Separate
2. Combine
3. Evaluate
4. Assign

*Now the earth was formless and empty,
darkness was over the surface of the deep,
and the Spirit of God was hovering over
the waters. And God said, "Let there be
light," and there was light. God saw that
the light was good, and he separated the
light from the darkness. (Genesis 1:2-4)*

On the first day of creation, the first step our Father
God took in creating order out of an empty earth
was to bring forth light and separate it from darkness.
When we begin to create order in our lives, we do the
same thing. First, start by separating the darkness—that

is, we identify those things that need to go into *dark* trash bags. Actually, we separate in three ways: the things we want to *keep* from those things we choose to *give away* or *throw away*.

Separate
A. Keep
B. Give away
C. Throw away

Let's start with *keep*. Pick up the first item and ask yourself if you really want to keep it. When is the last time you used it? The principles and rules in the following chapters will help guide you in making those decisions. Use some bright papers from the supply list (described in Chapter 12, "Basic Supplies") to make signs and identify the various items you want to keep. If you have something that needs to go to another area in your home, use a bright paper to designate it. For example, you might have papers that read: "Goes to garage"; "Bring to basement"; "Return to Ruth"; "Put in Patty's room"; "Carry to cleaners"; and "Ask Alan." Your "keep" stack should be relatively small compared to your give-away and throw-away bags.

Next, *give away*. Before starting the organizing process, find out what charities are nearby and what kind of items they can use. In Atlanta, my good friend Gayle is the Chaplain for a women's prison and work-release center. As I help clients clean out their closets, I take bags of useful and attractive clothes, shoes, purses, and personal and household items to Gayle, and she disperses them to the ladies who are looking for jobs and new homes. What a blessing—for them, my client, and me! Remember, however, that some of what you uncover is only junk, and junk needs to be thrown away. If you wouldn't pass it on to a friend you want to keep as a friend, then toss it. No one will miss it.

You will probably find items you want to give away to specific people. Set these in designated piles on the floor. Put most of the give-away piles close to you so it is easier to toss things into those piles. Take some sheets of brightly colored paper. Label each stack with a sheet of paper by writing the name or ministry with a magic marker. After a while, things will be spread out all over the floor, and the colors will help keep you focused. Don't be concerned about which color to use for different stacks. Pick any colors and duplicate them as needed. This is a time when you don't want to be too organized in your organizing.

As give-away items pile up, place them in bags marked with white labels and put them on the opposite side of the room from the trash bags. At the end of the day, tie a knot in the bags and move them to a holding area such as a basement or garage. Remember: Don't make the bags too heavy for you (or anyone else) to carry. Make a note to call those people by the next day so they know you have some things for them. Plan to have all the bags out of your house in no more than seven days.

Make a list of which bags go to particular people or organizations. Next to each entry on the list, mark the planned date of each drop-off or pick-up. Don't make the mistake of leaving these bags sitting around your house for months!

Finally, but most importantly, decide to *throw away.* You may be wondering, "How in the world do I throw away all these things I've been clinging to for years?" Some very helpful tips to help you make these decisions are in the following chapters.

Get ready to do some serious tossing. Make sure you have a trash can (approximately 2 ft. tall, the size of a tall kitchen garbage can) right next to you. If one is not available, a large shopping bag or a laundry basket will do. Put it on the side of your dominate hand to facilitate the active process of holding, thinking, and tossing. Make this as easy as possible so you can toss out as much as possible. Here's an effective method:

A. Hold and think for three to seven seconds.
B. Then, decide in three seconds.
C. Toss immediately.
D. Pick up more and toss again.
E. Toss more.
F. Toss even more.
G. Continue tossing.
H. Don't stop tossing!

At that rate, you can process 360 to 600 items in an uninterrupted hour. If you worked for a minimum of three hours, you would process 1,080 to 1,800 items. Is that possible? Those numbers are unrealistic, but the point is: The more you throw away, the easier and faster it goes. A common question to ask yourself is, "What is the worst that will happen if I throw it away?"

Place a large black or brown trash bag somewhere in the same room or near the door to empty the trash can when it gets full. As soon as the big trash bag is full—but not too heavy to carry easily (watch your back)—tie it up by rolling the top down, taking both ends, and tying a knot. A knotted bag is much harder to re-open than using twist ties. Take the bag outside to the garbage can immediately.

Honor your spouse and other family members. Always ask them about their own possessions. Be very cautious not to throw away their things without permission. If you are in doubt about an item, put it aside and ask them about it. When working in homes, I always have stacks of items labeled clearly with family members' names so we can ask them about their things. These people will appreciate your concern for their input and your respect for their treasures (no matter how junky they may be to us).

One of my clients, Renee, a school teacher in Easton, Maryland, was so excited about being free from the excess stuff in her attic that she stood on top of all of her 56 bags of trash while I took her picture! You'll be excited too, as you throw stuff away. The more you throw away, the easier it also is to give things away, and that's fun! It is a refreshing feeling!

Step 1: Separate

A. Keep
B. Give away
C. Throw away

Chapter 6
STEP TWO: COMBINE

1. Separate
2. Combine
3. Evaluate
4. Assign

And God said, "Let the water under the sky be gathered to one place, and let dry ground appear." And it was so. (Genesis 1:9)

When we gather things, we combine them. Our second step in organizing is to *combine* identical and similar items. First we separate out the things we want to keep, and then we begin to combine those "keep" items into similar categories. God combined water with water to make room for the land. We can make more room when we simply combine similar items.

Combine

A. Identical and similar items
B. Items into categories
C. Items often used together

For example, let's say you are organizing your kitchen. We open up the cabinet and see baking dishes, food, and cups all together on one shelf. Those are all different categories of items. Our goal is to combine similar items to save space, make things easier to find, and avoid confusion.

You may start with any item, but let's say you decide to start with the baking dishes. Separate the ones to keep, give away, and any old, cracked, or chipped ones to throw away. Be honest with yourself. If you are not using certain baking dishes, you may have too many in that size, you either never need them, or maybe you simply just don't like them.

Pick a spot on top of the counter, or preferably a nearby table, and designate that spot for combining the baking dishes you want to keep. When you are organizing a kitchen, the tops of counters and tables are where all of your "keep" items will be combined, so there is no need to mark it with a paper. If you are short on table and counter space, you can use clean laundry baskets lined with towels, in which case you'll need to label them "keep" with bright paper. Give-away items will go on the floor or in boxes.

Do the same thing with the cups. Separate the ones you really like and enjoy using. Put the "keep" cups in a different place on the counter from the baking dishes. Again, be honest. If you are not using some of them, you probably don't really like the shapes, colors, sizes, or feel. It's OK to give them away. Immediately put them into the "give away" stack on the floor.

Do the same thing with the food. Throw away all of the old food, and put the good food you want to keep in a designated "keep" spot on the counter or table. Also be sure to check the it's-old-but-I-think-it's-still-OK-food to see if it has any bugs. Now is a good time to rid your cabinets of all unwanted creatures. Look closely for little holes in bags, and watch for pieces of macaroni that move on their own!

Each of your stacks should have room to grow. Now, open up another cabinet. Yikes! More of the same! Don't panic, just go through the same process: Combine the food with the food stack, cups and eating dishes with the cup and dish pile, and baking dishes with the baking pile. Serving dishes go together; everyday eating dishes are separated from the nicer dishes or china; and glasses are put together.

When you pull something out of the cabinet, combine it with a similar type of item. If you run out of sorting space altogether, start putting things back into the cabinets into the places you think you will want them, but keep an open mind to make changes as you proceed throughout the whole kitchen.

As your piles increase, you may be surprised at just how much of everything you have. Now is the best time to separate items once and for all. When you see that you have twelve Tupperware™ bowls all the same size, and only seven of them have lids, now is the time to give away at least five or more of them.

For most of my clients, getting their Tupperware™ organized has been one of their greatest joys. The task often appears overwhelming at first because plastic containers and lids are everywhere, but when they follow this process of *separating* and *combining,* they finally can see what they actually had—and didn't need.

Many years ago, I was privileged to help my wonderful sister, Terri, organize her kitchen. (If you are close to your family and get along well, you can be a great source of help and encouragement to one another. But help each other only if you can accept one another just as you are.) She used her Tupperware™ every day for her husband and daughters' lunches. It was a source of daily irritation to find the right container and then find the lid that fit.

Terri and I gave away the odd pieces and combined the similar sizes together along with other lunch-making containers. Small containers were stacked in a small plastic basket with all the lids that fit those sizes neatly in the same basket. The larger containers went into a larger plastic basket. These were put in the cabinet where she liked to make lunches, so all she had to do in the mornings was pull out the two baskets. Everything she needed was together, lids and all.

Also, when Terri's husband and daughters cleaned up the kitchen, they knew exactly where the Tupperware™ went, so bowls and lids were no longer scattered all over the kitchen. As you can imagine, lunch-making went from being a chore to a joy. Terri's Tupperware™ cabinet has stayed organized all these years, as well as the rest of her kitchen. When guests are helping in the kitchen, they invariably admire the neat-ness and order, with exclamations of how great her Tupperware™ looks.

While organizing any area, the same rule applies: Combine identical items. The most efficient way to com-bine similar items is to do so while you are separating your "keep" items like Terri did. However, if your work space is tight, and depending on the type of item you are organizing, you may have to accomplish the combining process in stages, once the decisions for separating are complete. For example, when you are organizing a closet, designate areas on the bed with different bright papers for your specific types of clothes: dress, casual, and work. The give-away pile will be on the floor on the opposite side of the room from the trash bag. As you make deci-sions about the clothes you want to keep, begin to combine them in designated piles. However, in a small bedroom with a twin bed, use the available room by piling up all the "keep" clothes, and emptying the closet. After you take out the trash and give-away bags, put a sheet on the floor and spread out different categories of clothes, combining similar types. Clothes will need to be even further separated by categories such as women's skirts from jackets. I usually split up women's suits to enable us to mix and match outfits better. Combine men's short-sleeve shirts, long-sleeve shirts, casual shirts, jeans, and casual pants from dressy casual pants. Keep men's suits together. Combine those hundreds of men's hats, and give many of them away—with permission, of course.

These steps work in every area you are organizing, no matter what it is or where it is. You are doing great so far! Keep moving and proceed to the third step.

STEP 2: COMBINE

A. Identical and similar items
B. Items into categories
C. Items often used together

Chapter 7
STEP THREE: EVALUATE

1. Separate
2. Combine
*3. **Evaluate***
4. Assign

*God called the dry ground "land," and the
gathered waters he called "seas." And God
saw that it was good. (Genesis 1:10)*

To determine if something is good or not, we have to
stand back, look at it carefully, and *evaluate* it. God
must have done the same thing when He looked at His
work of creating on that third day and "saw that it was
good."

Let's see if our work so far is good. Look over the
different "combined" piles of items on the floor, tables, or
counters and first make positively sure you want to keep
the things in each stack. Now *evaluate* them in terms of

high and low priority, which in organizing actually means *high and low usage*, or perhaps, *no more usage*.

> Evaluate
> A. High and low priority
> B. High and low usage
> C. No more usage

Ask yourself, "How often am I using this item? Is it something I use frequently or occasionally? Is it only a seasonal item? When was the last time I used it?"

Begin to pull out the *high usage* items from one stack. The things left in that stack should be your *low usage* items. Now reconsider if the low usage items are really important to you. Perhaps they are just taking up unnecessary space. Some will continue to be very important, but they aren't used frequently.

A large, beautiful serving dish in the kitchen may be your favorite, but it may be so large that it is only used when entertaining many guests, which for you, might not be that often. A certain tool in your workshop may be of great importance, but only used when you make certain wood creations. These things would be *low priority, low usage* even though they are important to keep. However, for the person who frequently entertains large groups, or who uses the tool often for repairs, these items would be *high priority, high usage*.

But that dish which hasn't been used in twelve years, and the tool that is so old, dull, rusted, and broken that you'll never be able to use again, need to go. Face it.

These are your *no more usage* items, and they need to be separated out into the darkness of the dump. Be honest with yourself about these things.

In the early days of my organizing before I learned to ask all the right questions, I worked with Andi, a delightful lady with a great sense of humor who lives in Greenville, South Carolina. We were organizing her kitchen when we got to the very top cabinets—you know, the ones high above the normal cabinets—where things get stored and are never seen again. I climbed up and began to pull out about 50 to 60 baby food jars so she could make decisions on whether to keep them or not. When she said, "Keep," I assumed that since her children were grown she must use them for making jelly.

Later, when we began the evaluation process, I asked her when was the last time she used the jars. She confessed it had been about 19 years. She had not used them since her children outgrew baby food. We had a good laugh together, and she realized that she had been "holding onto" her children by holding onto these jars. We stopped and prayed together that she would be able to "let go" of her children and entrust them into the hands of God. That day was a day of release in her. Only God could have known that cleaning out baby food jars would have a profound impact on her life.

As you evaluate high and low usage items, be honest with yourself and you will be ready for the next step: *Assign.*

STEP 3: EVALUATE

A. High and low priority

B. High and low usage

C. No more usage

Chapter 8
STEP FOUR: ASSIGN

GP

1. Separate
2. Combine
3. Evaluate
4. Assign

Then God said, "Let the land produce vegetation: seed-bearing plants and trees on the land that bear fruit with seed in it, according to their various kinds." And it was so. The land produced vegetation: plants bearing seed according to their kinds and trees bearing fruit with seed in it according to their kinds. And God saw that it was good. And there was evening, and there was morning—the third day. (Genesis 1:11-13)

Now God begins planting His garden with the vegetation, plants, and trees. He *assigns* them to a specific place—the land. We take for granted that trees don't float on water, nor do plants grow in mid-air.

Everything has its place and living things reproduce according to their kind. There is no confusion, and there are no mishaps. God's clear, workable plan is taking shape.

Your plan of organizing will begin to come together as you *assign* places for all of your "keep" items. We *assign* a place for everything based on our *evaluation* of the *combined* stacks of similar items, those things we have *separated* and fully determined to keep as outlined in the previous three steps.

First, evaluate the spaces you have just cleaned out. Determine which space is *high priority, high usage* space. That would be the space most accessible to you and the easiest to retrieve based on height, length, location, and its relationship to all the other spaces. In an office, the highest priority space would be the file drawer in your desk. Lowest priority would be the file cabinet across the room.

Next, look at your *high usage items* and match them into the *high usage spaces.* Continue to do this with all of your goods. Once your high priority items are in their place, you can put the low priority items into the backs of shelves, drawers, closets, and corners. The end result is that you have automatically assigned the most important places for the most frequently used items. Everything you use all the time should now be at your fingertips, or at least very easy to reach.

A very important point to remember here is to *customize* and *assign* things to places that work best for you.

Be creative. Don't think you should only put things where someone told you they should go. Experiment as you assign items on shelves, hang clothes on racks, lay things in drawers, and put papers in files. Give yourself permission to change your mind as many times as you like. Your system probably won't be perfect and won't be exactly what you want on the first attempts.

Assign a Place for Everything Based on:
A. Putting high usage items into high usage spaces
B. Putting low usage items into low usage spaces
C. Customizing what works best for you

When assigning places, give yourself license to try new things, no matter how unusual or out of character it may seem. Change it after you get to another area, and then try something else. This step is the most enjoyable, and it is the easiest of all. Make it fun! Finish one area, keep moving, and then come back as you get new ideas. Let your imagination roll.

I tell my clients to think of the assigning step like a rough draft when writing an important letter, paper, or proposal. Write the first draft, make changes, re-write it, and make changes again. You may write many drafts before you are happy with the finished product. Assigning is the same way. You may put certain items on a shelf in the closet, but as you continue to organize, you may change your mind and move them to another shelf. Don't try to think it through too much. Just start assigning places as you go, knowing that you have the liberty to make changes. Pray and ask God to show you where to put things. He may give you new ideas which you've never considered before.

Once you have some goods in place, stop and close the drawers and doors. Walk out of the room. Now, pretend you are just walking in to retrieve a particular item. Test and see how easy it is to reach for, get to, pull out, set down, put on, and put back. If it doesn't seem to flow naturally, try something different.

Remember: Even when you are through organizing, you still will be making minor changes periodically in your assignment of items, so don't make the mistake of trying to make everything completely perfect. As you use certain goods, you may find they work better if assigned to different areas from your original plans. Always be willing to change. One of the secrets to getting organized and staying organized is the willingness to change. Enjoy the opportunity to change, and you will always have fun making new decisions when you are assigning things to particular places.

The most important secret for getting organized and staying organized is to accomplish the four steps *in their order.* Follow each step thoroughly and deliberately. Don't skip around, and above all, don't work on the last step first!

Catch yourself. Nearly every time I organize people, they come to an item, and their first thought is, "I don't know where to put this." When you find you are assigning first, stop and remind yourself to *first* separate, combine, evaluate, and *then* assign. You may need to re-train your thinking.

Applying these Four Steps in order is the most important lesson of all!

As you are getting ready to organize, open the book to this chapter, keep it open and in front of you at all times as a constant reminder. When things get overwhelming and confusing, look at the next page and then, if necessary, refer back to the chapter on that particular step for more details. These steps will enable you to organize every area of your life from the smallest detail to the largest project.

Learn them well, say them out loud, and memorize them in order: Separate, Combine, Evaluate, Assign. Then commit to memory each step with the ABC's.

THE MOST IMPORTANT SECRET FOR GETTING ORGANIZED AND STAYING ORGANIZED IS TO ACCOMPLISH THESE STEPS IN ORDER:

1. Separate
   A. Keep
   B. Give away
   C. Throw away

2. Combine
   A. Identical and similar items
   B. Items into categories
   C. Items often used together

3. Evaluate
   A. High and low priority
   B. High and low usage
   C. No more usage

4. Assign a Place for Everything Based on:
   A. Putting high usage items into high usage spaces
   B. Putting low usage items into low usage spaces
   C. Customizing what works best for you

Chapter 9
WHERE DO I START?

GP

Where do you start? *With prayer.* Ask God to give you wisdom about where to start. He knows what you need. He knows what the future holds and what events are going to be the most important in the days to come. Does He seem to be impressing you with some urgency about a particular area? If so, that is definitely the place to start.

You may be thinking, "I'm feeling a strong desire to start in this particular area, but I don't know why. It doesn't make sense." Go with what you believe God is leading you to do, even if you don't understand the reason. God directs each of us individually and uniquely. Just because a friend started organizing in the kitchen doesn't necessarily mean that's the best place for you to start. The changes God is making in your friend's life may be very different from the changes He wants to make in your life.

If you pray about it and still don't get a sense of where to start, then ask yourself, *"What area is producing the most anxiety or making me irritable?"* When I am designing a plan of action with my clients, they can always answer that question. That area is often the place to start, no matter how illogical it may seem. In the process of organizing, you may be impressed to do some illogical things in making decisions about where to start or what to do with a particular item. At the time, these impressions don't make sense, but later, you will understand. Only God knows what is ahead for you, and He may speak to you by simply giving you a strong desire to start organizing in a certain area of your life.

If you are organizing on your own, I normally recommend that you do not start in your closet unless God is particularly leading you to start there. The closet is the hardest place to organize. Why? Because that is where a lot of our emotions are stored.

Our closets are full of clothes that tell us we have gained weight or that remind us of when we were sick and lost weight. They are full of memories of good times long past . . . or painful times that still haunt us. Closets are often filled with guilt because they contain clothes with tags still on them that we never should have bought, and we feel guilty. We can't take them back, but we spent a lot of money on them, so we'll just let them hang there even though they really don't fit. We may be hoarding old clothes we've been hanging onto for years and years and years. We can't get rid of them because they are a part of us, yet we don't wear them because they are worn out, ugly, and out of style. Sometimes clothes remind us of situations which have been terribly painful. And then there are all those shoes that don't fit! When we are hanging onto anything, particularly clothes, shoes, hats, and men's caps, it usually indicates we are hanging onto some inner clutter. We may have a lot of old stuff within us that God desires to cleanse so we can be set free. That's why praying about it first is so important. God always has the most effective agenda for us.

In one series on personal organization I did in Atlanta, I gave homework as usual and explained to everyone that the closet was the hardest place to organize and not to start there, unless of course, they were feeling especially led by God to do so. They had a week before the next session. One young couple, Ben and Lydia, were attending the seminar together and went home so excited about getting started. After praying about it, they began that very night while their two small children were asleep. Ben started in his workroom and eventually went to bed. Lydia, however, went immediately to her closet and began to clean out and throw away stuff. The next week, Lydia candidly shared her experience with the rest of the group. She explained that at 4:00 A.M. in the morning, Ben got up and came into the closet. He wondered why his precious wife was still up. Lydia was sitting on the floor in the middle of the closet, crying her eyes out. She had been sitting there crying for hours and hours.

God was leading her to start in her closet because He had a cleansing work He wanted to do inside her. Many items were stored in her closet which were associated with her Dad, who had passed away. Grief over his death had strained relationships with the rest of her family. All night long, Lydia pulled out clothes and belongings, processing that grief. Only God knew she still needed that cleansing work accomplished in her heart.

While I don't recommend staying up all night to clean out your closet, it worked in this particular case. With two small children underfoot, Lydia had never allowed herself to "let go." In the middle of the night, she had the freedom to cry and allow the Lord to heal her. The next day, she felt like a new person, and Ben noticed a new calmness and peace in his beloved wife. A key here is that Ben was incredibly understanding and supportive of his wife's feelings. This experience strengthened their relationship, and they have openly shared their story numerous times to the benefit of others.

A special note: if you are working with a Professional Organizer, the closet sometimes is the *best* place to start. I instruct my clients to utilize my talents in their most difficult areas. The skills and principles they will learn while we are working together will equip them to work in other areas on their own.

Whether working alone or with help, just remember: Always start with prayer, and you'll be off to a good start.

WHERE DO I START?

A. Where? With prayer.

B. Ask: "What area is producing anxiety?"

C. And ask: "What makes me feel irritable?"

Chapter 10
WHEN DO I START?

*N*ow. There's no better time. Don't put it off, and don't make excuses for delay. When people have expressed their need to get organized, they have remarked to me, "I'm feeling convicted about the clutter in my life, and I *have to* do something about it!" If you are feeling that sense of urgency, it may be God's leading in preparation for a change or event in your life. Sometimes He is getting ready to bless you, and He wants you to be in the position to fully enjoy the blessing.

This was true of Elizabeth, who faithfully attended nine months of my Sunday School classes on *Organizing—A Biblical Perspective.* She was feeling that "push" to clean out and organize her lovely home in Roswell, Georgia. Nearly every week she put into practice the steps and principles she was learning. Prior to these classes, she had taken an early retirement from her executive position with a major corporation in Atlanta. She had been traveling and praying about the next position. A number of lucrative offers started coming in from different firms around the country, but something kept tugging at her heart, including the urgency to purge her twenty-seven years' accumulation of things so she could find order and peace.

God led Elizabeth to a two-year commitment with a ministry in Tallahassee, Florida, where she is happier and more fulfilled than she ever was in her corporate position. With newly acquired organizing skills, she was able to clean out all the excess in her life and lighten her load. She purged, threw away, gave away, and loaned out much of her furniture to friends, who, in each remarkable case, had just moved or experienced a change in which they suddenly had empty rooms in their homes and needed additional furniture. She jokingly referred to these situations as her "rooms-to-go." She loaned them nearly everything in each room of her house. With beaming eyes, she often told her story of how she previously held onto nearly everything in her life, but now she was no longer a prisoner of her things. What a great example of someone set free!

Don't delay. Start somewhere. Even if it is something small, like one drawer or one shelf of books. It may seem to be insignificant, but a small, successful beginning may be the key to the rest of your organizing project. Deliberately taking that first step will help you overcome the inertia of starting.

Have you ever noticed how procrastination can quickly make even a small project into a foreboding impossibility? The idea of organizing your entire home or office may seem overwhelming, but attack it in the same way as you would eat an elephant: *one bite at the time.* Start and don't stop. Take it a bite (or a step) at a time. Let this book help you stay on track. Get some help if you need it, and read this book again. Taking even one small bite out of your clutter is a big step in the right direction.

No matter where I am, the subject of organizing often pops up because most people struggle with this issue on some level. When I dine with friends, they sometimes feel a pressing need to explain where they are in terms of order and clutter in their home or office. I always enjoy talking about this highly varied and interesting topic, and I've learned some insightful ideas during some of those dinners. A number of years ago, several of my friends simultaneously had a peculiar urgency to clean out their basements. They each procrastinated, saying they were just "too busy" to deal with all that clutter, but ironically, within twelve months every one of them had flooding in their basements. Then they were forced to clean out their basements, and wow, what a mess they were! Here are some of their stories.

During one of our few and unexpected freezes in Atlanta, my friends Vincent and Dottie had a basement pipe freeze and break while they were out of town. Before they returned, the weather warmed (as it always does in the South), and they came home to a basement full of water. They placed an urgent call to me, and I appeared with wet-vac and a big box of black trash bags in hand. It was harder work since we had to get up the water in the entire basement in only a few hours, and now we had much more work trying to dry salvageable items. We had no time to waste on decision-making with boxes dripping wet, so it forced our decisions of what to throw away.

My friend Andrea lived in an older home in a quaint section of the city. She had one of those memorable basements that always fondly reminded me of the basement at Noono's, my Italian Grandfather in New York. You may know that smell—old, musty, with every nook and cranny filled with something "I can use one of these days." Andrea and I frequently laughed together about "the need to do something with all that stuff down there," but when we got together, we weren't interested in organizing. We were intent on eating. That year, we had record rainfall, and water poured from her backyard, down her drive, and through the basement door. She frantically called me—along with a few good men—to move the heavy furniture, and I came running with wet-vac and black garbage bags. We worked hard and fast, and the curb was lined with garbage bags by the end of that long, long day. There was so much trash, the neighbors thought she was moving .

Tom and Lacy had a similar experience. Their flood forced them to clean out all the boxes they brought into their marriage. A couple in their 40's, they both had been previously married to spouses who had passed away. Tom and Lacy had been happily married three years when I first met them. They were living in a fairly new home in Washington, D.C. Their flood was not as severe, but it was enough to force them to unpack china and other items. This work reminded them of old wounds and memories, and the process opened more communication between them. Discussing their feelings about their pasts strengthened their marriage.

Then there was my own basement. When I first moved to Gainesville, Georgia, in 1991, I set up my office in the finished basement of my condo. I had boxes and boxes of books sitting on the floor, waiting to be purged. On the morning of Good Friday, I walked downstairs to eight inches of water! The pipe coming into my condo from the main line outside had burst and water was pouring through my basement, out the sliding glass doors, down the hill in the back, and into Lake Lanier below. An urgent call to my friends, who by now jokingly referred to me as the "wet-vac bag lady," urged them to come running with helping hands. I also learned my own lesson in procrastination. I threw away many books that I really didn't need anyway, but the job would have been much easier if I had only taken one bite at a time and purged a box of books every day!

The point is: *The sooner you get going, the easier it will be.* It's really not hard; it's just a matter of getting started. You won't always know what to do, how to do it, or have all the answers in advance. If you use these simple principles and steps, you'll be surprised at how much you'll learn along the way. It will take some time, but make up your mind and start *now.*

When Do I Start?

A. Now! Don't delay.

B. It's OK, take a small bite at a time.

C. The sooner you get going, the easier it will be.

Chapter 11
GET READY TO GET ORGANIZED

$\boxed{\text{GP}}$

G et ready and get excited about the challenge ahead of you! As you approach your beginning date of organizing, a few steps of advance preparation will help you be more focused and productive. Go over the following points with each member of your family, or if you are working in an office, with your staff. These steps are all very important to the success of your project. Take each one seriously and follow them carefully.

The best preparation for getting organized
is prayer and time in the Word.

1. Pray. Nothing can replace the power of prayer.

2. Ask others to pray. Intercessory prayer is very important. Order is of God, and getting organized is in obedience to His will, which is always best for you. Disorder causes a lot of confusion, and confusion comes from the one who is against God. When you are organizing,

you are battling against the enemy of our souls, the author of confusion. You will need the help of others who are faithful to pray. If you don't know of anyone who can pray for you, put forth the extra effort to find and involve praying people in your life. Ask God to show you someone! He is always faithful to answer. The apostle Paul wrote to the believers in Philippi, "And my God will meet all your needs according to his glorious riches in Christ Jesus" (Philippians 4:19).

3. Study the first chapter of Genesis in the Bible, and ask God to prepare your heart. Your time in God's Word will give you an extra measure of understanding, knowledge, strength, and sensitivity to God's will. He knows everything and will guide and direct you to make the best use of your time.

4. Get plenty of rest the night before you start. Organizing can be exhausting. You will be making a lot of decisions, and you need to be alert.

5. Don't stay up late cleaning the night before you start organizing. You will be making a mess as you pull things out in organizing. Don't waste your time and your energy cleaning first.

6. As you organize, have a few cleaning rags handy to wipe down the dust along the way. If you will be organizing bookshelves or de-cluttering dressers, have some

furniture polish ready. For kitchens, have a few cleansers and cleaning rags out and ready to use. It is important to clean as you go before setting items on shelves and surface tops; but remember to keep your energy focused on organizing, not cleaning. This is *not* the time to do the baseboards just because it's the first time you've seen them in a while! You will be able to thoroughly clean later once things are completely organized.

7. At least several days in advance, get your basic supplies ready. (See the list in Chapter 12, "Basic Supplies.") Don't wait until the day before you organize to go to the store! If unexpected interruptions occur and prevent you from shopping on that one day, you'll be unprepared!

8. Focus your attention on the task at hand. Plan to avoid answering the phones. Turn on the message recorder. In an office, be prepared to have calls held while you are working. Important calls can be returned during breaks.

9. Be realistic about the time it will take. Most people who have gone through the process will tell you, "It takes four to five times longer to organize than I thought it would take." Disorder didn't happen overnight—neither will organizing. Be prepared to spend the necessary time to finish the process.

10. Dress casually and comfortably. You will work better if you are not afraid of sitting down on the floor to sort items.

11. Develop a "roll up your sleeves" attitude. Dig into those piles, keep working, and expect results.

12. Stretch those muscles. You will be stretching your brain making many decisions, and your muscles can use a good stretch, too. Prepare to take *short* stretch breaks in the beginning and every two hours or whenever you need to. This exercise will be good for your circulation. It will keep the blood flowing and the brain working better.

13. If you will be working all day, plan to take a lunch hour away from the work, but eat lightly. Go to another room, an office, or somewhere off the premises. Don't eat lunch where you are organizing! You need to get away and come back refreshed with new insight and ideas.

14. Have a large plastic water bottle nearby and drink lots of water. Don't drink much caffeine. Protect your blood sugar level from a roller-coaster ride so you'll have much more energy and stamina. Absolutely, positively, drink no alcohol at all. Alcohol and organizing do not mix.

15. Eat protein energy snacks, not sugar snacks. I often bring dry-roasted nuts, raisins, fruit, soy nuts, or yogurt to snack on while I'm working, and I eat just a little bit every now and then. But snacking is not an excuse for stopping! Keep moving, unless you are taking a much needed break.

16. When you first start to feel the need to take a break, do it then. You probably need it. Stop, look at the clock, give yourself ten to fifteen minutes. Time it and stick to it. Walk away from the area where you are working. Freshen up your water. Have a snack. Stretch. Go outside if the weather permits, and take some deep breaths. Look up and thank God for the opportunity to get organized.

17. Many people who get organized will tell you, "It gets worse before it gets better." Expect things to look very messy in the process, as all the clutter is brought to the surface. Take heart! It *will* come together.

18. If someone will be working with you, discuss in advance how you can best work together as a team. Do you want help with the initial planning? Do you want help with the actual decision making for each item? Do you want the person's assistance from beginning to end or just at certain times in the process? Make it very clear to the other person what you expect from him or her.

19. All your organizing ideas are important. Even a simple thought can be a springboard for new and better ideas. Have a letter-size tablet or clipboard with blank paper handy to make notes and draft different ideas until the process is fine-tuned. Remember that you'll be customizing what works best for you to stay organized. (See Chapter 8, "Step Four: Assign.")

20. Tell others about your plans to organize. Most people feel free to share with friends and family that they are getting more organized to better themselves. Other people are usually quite impressed with your commitment, and they will respect you for the determination and tenacity it takes. However, take care to share only with ones who are supportive. You don't need any criticism or sarcasm at this point!

21. Spend a little bit of time planning. (See Chapter 14, "Your Plan of Action.")

22. Schedule a baby-sitter for the children in a separate location from your home. As precious as they are, it doesn't work to try and organize with little ones in the same house, no matter how big the house is. All you will accomplish by trying to manage children while you organize is building the level of your frustration. Trust me on this one.

23. Be prepared by thoroughly reading Chapters 5 through 8 on the four steps of organization and follow those steps in their order.

24. Most importantly, get ready by going over this list in advance of beginning the process of organizing. The more prepared you are, the more efficient start you will have. All the steps are important to your success. Start out by asking God for help. He is faithful to help you because organizing always brings us into a closer relationship with Him.

Remember:

The best preparation
for getting organized
is
prayer and time in the Word.

Chapter 12
BASIC SUPPLIES:
FIREWOOD AND MATCHES
OR BOXES AND TRASH BAGS?

GP

When God told Abraham to sacrifice his only son whom he loved, Abraham didn't procrastinate. He immediately obeyed by saddling his donkey early the next morning and leaving on this difficult journey. But first he gathered everything he would need to accomplish the task God had given him.

When he had cut enough wood for the burnt offering, he set out for the place God had told him about. (Genesis 22:3)

If Abraham's intent was to avoid obeying God, he wouldn't have gotten the supplies ready. However, he was serious in his obedience to God and was fully prepared by cutting "enough wood for the burnt offering." Read this popular and wonderfully inspirational story in Genesis 22:1-19.

When you and I are getting organized, we need to be prepared to sacrifice some things in our lives that are creating physical, spiritual, and emotional clutter. Just as God provided a lamb for the burnt offering in place of Isaac, He will also provide healing for our spiritual and emotional clutter. But if we are serious about cleaning out the physical clutter, we don't need wood, unless we are planning a big bonfire as many of my clients have jokingly requested to burn all their stuff! They didn't even want to sort it.

We must be prepared in advance with enough supplies, beginning with plenty of large, opaque black or brown trash bags. Obviously, we (and others in our households) don't need to see the things we have thrown away. If we can see them after we've thrown them away, these discarded things stand too good a chance of being rescued and put back into the closet! Buy a big box (50-count or more) and make double sure they are thick (1.1 mil.) so trash won't be scattering through the neighborhood from broken bags.

The list below includes additional provisions to begin your journey in organizing. If your budget is tight, at least start with the first four most vital items, and get some used boxes for heavy give-away items.

1. Large (30-Gal.), thick (1.1mil.), black or brown opaque trash bags, at least 50-count.

2. One package of assorted, brightly colored 8-1/2" x 11" paper (50 or more sheets).

3. Several black magic markers. (When one is misplaced, you don't want to waste time looking for it.)

4. Plastic zipper-type bags in these sizes: 2 gallon, 1 gallon, and 1 quart. Buy one box of each to start. Some people use only a few of these bags, but others go through several boxes.

5. Plastic storage containers, found in discount stores: The sizes and number of containers you should purchase varies widely depending on the size of your organizing project, the storage space needed for unused containers while you are organizing, sales prices, and your budget. A good general rule is to begin with the most commonly used boxes in these approximate sizes:

A. Small, shoe box size (6 quart or 14"L x 8"W x 4.5"H). Start with about one dozen.

B. Medium container (15 quart or 17"L x 11"W x 6.5"H). Get about one dozen.

C. Large container (56 quart, or 14 gallon, or 22"L x 16"W x 11"H). You may not need this larger size, but when organizing in the home, you will probably need at least several, especially if you are storing clothes.

Plan on spending some extra time looking at the many different shapes, sizes, and colors available, and choose any other containers that you like. I recommend clear boxes for most items so you can see the items stored in them, particularly for children. Check the lids, and be sure they open and close easily. Make sure the container feels good and is comfortable to handle. You have to *like* the box to enjoy using it!

Remember to keep your receipt. Most stores will refund your money if you don't need them all. (Although in all these years of organizing, I've seldom had a client return any containers. Most of them needed to purchase many more.)

6. New cardboard storage boxes (12"W x 10"H x 15"L): These boxes are found in office supply stores, usually packed several flat to a package and are very easy to put together. They are great to store papers and other items in attics, garages, and dry basements since they are small enough to handle and stack well.

7. One package of large white labels (2" x 4" size is best) for bags and containers. You may choose to type labels on the computer or use an electronic label maker, but handwritten ones are just fine.

8. Several packages of 3" x 3" sticky-notes.

9. Be sure to stop and pick up some used boxes from the store to use for heavy and breakable give-away items.

These supplies are the very basics you'll need, and the quantities listed are just enough to get you started. They can be used for a wide variety of items in every room in your home and in every part of your office. As you organize, make a list of the different items and containers you need for specific purposes. Many of your needs can't be determined until you discover just how much you are keeping, what things need to be contained to keep them orderly, and the size of the areas where they will be stored. Write down the measurements of the spaces where you need to put a container. As you shop, carry a small measuring tape with you since the container labels don't always have the size of the container listed.

If you live a long distance away from a discount store, you may wish to purchase many containers in advance. Be sure to keep that receipt!

When you aren't sure what you need for storing a particular item, write down the item and the measurement of the space it takes. Get creative while you shop, and find something you like and would enjoy using to fit the necessary space. Have fun with this, and experiment until you seem to have a "good fit."

Finally, plan to purchase your supplies at least several days in advance. Don't wait until the day before you organize to go to the store. If unexpected interruptions occur and prevent you from shopping on that one day, you will be unprepared!

The night before you start organizing, get in "ready mode." Stack the supplies in an orderly manner, and you will be ready to roll up those sleeves!

Chapter 13
THE THREE-IN-ONE PRINCIPLE

GP

We begin organizing with a commitment to the Three-in-One Principle: *For every three things I own, I only need one.* This may sound a little extreme, but think about it. A primary reason we are disorganized is because we have too much stuff. The one and only way to begin the organizing process is by getting rid of the excess.

Look closely at what you really need. In the early days of organizing, I couldn't understand why some of my clients stayed organized while others went right back into their pattern of messy clutter. I began to see that the ones who stayed organized were the same ones who had thrown away the most stuff. Face it. Organizing your life simply will not work until you are willing to let go of some things.

Some of my clients have down-sized from very large homes to much smaller homes and quite literally gotten rid of two-thirds of their belongings in the process. They experience more freedom than any other people I know. They are happy and debt-free. That "heaviness" of being burdened by so many things is gone, and they are joyful. God is using them mightily everywhere they go. When we unload the excess in our lives, God does something very important in and through us.

In getting to know our Creator better, we can begin to deal with that inner clutter—the jumbled, painful emotional stuff that is going on inside of us. The clutter inside of us can be: bitterness; anger; resentment; unforgiveness; and often grief upon grief upon more grief: things that should have been but were not; things that we treasured but are now lost.

What happens when people don't know Him? They don't have the Holy Spirit to show them what is really going on with the inner clutter so they can resolve it and then bring the outer clutter into order. Still, some unbelievers follow Biblical principles, and God honors His Word whether they know Him or not. His principles stand firm.

One of the secrets to getting organized and staying organized is understanding the importance of throwing away and giving away, and making a firm commitment to the Three-in-One Principle. Make this commitment before going any further!

THE THREE-IN-ONE PRINCIPLE

For every three things I own,
I only need one.

Chapter 14
YOUR PLAN OF ACTION

GP

S hort, salty, and simple. That's how your organizing plan should be. A plan to get organized is different from other types of project planning. Don't let your plan be too long, involved, or detailed, because most of us don't really know what's lurking behind that closet door, under the bed, or in the attic. Even what appears on the outside to be a small hall closet or file drawer can mysteriously turn out piles and piles and piles of long-forgotten fossils of junk.

A. Make your plan *short, concise, and to the point. Write it down.* The purpose of the plan is to keep you focused and on task. It will remind you to keep moving, to stop reading the magazines you are sorting, and to make decisions quickly. A short, written plan will help you chart your course and prevent you from drowning in the sea of confusion surrounding your disorder. The points below will help you in writing your plan.

B. Add *salt* to your plan. Salt has many purposes, including seasoning and preserving food. *Season your organizing plan with humor*, and it will preserve your sanity. Like many recipes which call for a "pinch" of salt, even a little bit will make a big difference. A pinch of salt is much like little seeds and reminds me of the first time I ever planted a garden. In 1975, I moved from the big city of Atlanta to an old country farmhouse in the quaint, little north Georgia town of Clarkesville. That first summer, I excitedly learned all about gardening and canning. When I first planted my garden, however, I honestly couldn't believe that those little seeds were going to grow up into vegetable-producing plants, so I put out many extra seeds, just for good measure. Wow! Did my garden grow!

Your planning should be like that. Plant a few seeds of humor in your answers below to enable you to grow past the frustration and produce the fruit of order in your life.

C. Focus on *simple* questions with *simple* answers. Don't be too detailed or too thoughtful. Be *prayerful* and light-hearted. God created humor for a reason.

Now, get a full-size, 8.5" x 11" blank sheet of paper, and write out the following plan. This sample is from the plan I used for organizing a kitchen for Michael and Carolann, a couple with a great sense of humor who live in Chesapeake, Virginia, with their precious little girl, Kerri.

Organizing Plan for _the Kitchen_

Now answer these five key questions:
1. When do you plan to organize?

Day _Thursday_ Date _March 22_ Time _9:00 AM-5:00PM_
Day _Friday_ Date _March 23_ Time _9:00 AM-5:00PM_
Day _Monday_ Date _March 26_ Time _9:00 AM-2:00PM_

2. What area in this room/office produces anxiety?
The pantry.

3. What in this area causes irritation?
Getting my morning coffee—everything is scattered.

4. What is the most important thing I want to accomplish in this room/office?
My husband loves to cook pancakes on Saturdays for the family. I want all the things he uses to be together so it is easy for him and so he'll still be whistling when we sit down to eat.

5. What are the needs of other family or staff members in this room/office?
My daughter Kerri needs to have the cups she uses within reach so she won't have to continue jumping on top of the counter.

There you have it. From this very simple plan, I was able to learn a lot about this family. We began organizing and worked through the first three steps. When we reached Step Four, Assign, we first focused on assigning places for the pancake pan, bowl, utensils, and ingredients, as well as Kerri's cups. When we finished organizing Carolann's kitchen, the whole family was happy. And because the new system worked, the kitchen stayed organized. Since that day, they have put things back where they belonged.

The point is not that a plan is air-tight and fool-proof, but simply that you have a plan that works for you and your family. Make sure you accomplish your goal, and goals are different for different people. Your most important goal in organizing might be finding old tax records, making it easy to retrieve certain tapes, more room to exercise, less frustration in cooking, ease in finding the right tie in the morning, simplifying your mix & match outfits, or enabling the children to pick up their toys and to dress on time.

Be adaptable. Your plan needs to be very flexible. It will change as you go, so plan to change! Your written plan is simply a map to help you get where you want to go. You may decide to take a different route along the way, and that's fine.

Define, but don't refine your plan too much. In other words: Don't spend all your time planning. Taking time to write a detailed plan can be an excuse to avoid digging into the piles of clutter. One of my clients, Kelly, is a master planner and a successful entrepreneur. He and his wife, Sarah, live in San Francisco with their two teenage children, Mark and Beth. When I worked with Kelly and his staff in the company he owns, we spent the last few minutes of each organizing session to carefully plan our next area of attack.

I usually arrived on the specified day energized, excited, and ready to dive in, but Kelly often stopped me and insisted on going back over our plan of action. He then tried to discuss at great length how we were going to execute each and every detail, which in organizing, must be flexible because every situation is different. Instead of making progress purging, he preferred to plan.

The other extreme is Philip, who lives in Los Angeles. He resisted any kind of planning and jumped from one area to another in the middle of organizing. With his great sense of humor, however, we both laughed when I tried to stop him to get him re-focused.

A good example of a balance between these two extremes is Kelly's wife, Sarah. I worked with Sarah and their children in their home. Sarah and I usually spent three to seven minutes planning the next day of organizing, and when I arrived, she was ready. The supplies were purchased and stacked neatly near the room where we were organizing. Often she was already in the midst of purging! We worked hard, Sarah made quick decisions, and we accomplished a lot each day. We seldom planned the next step until we were finished with each area because we often changed our minds in the process. Having a room in order always gives people a new perspective and new priorities.

Remember: Don't try to orchestrate the perfect plan. It will never be perfect. Organizing is unpredictable. Just write down answers to the Five Key Questions, and you'll be on the right course!

Now it's your turn. Write out your own plan on the following page:

Organizing Plan for _____

1. I plan to organize on the following dates:

Day_____ Date _____ Time _____

Day_____ Date _____ Time _____

Day_____ Date _____ Time _____

2. What area in this room/office produces anxiety?

3. What in this area causes irritation?

4. What is the most important thing I want to accomplish in this room/office?

5. What are the needs of other family or staff members in this room/office? Your Plan of Action

Your Plan of Action

A. Short. Make your plan short, concise, and to the point. Write it down.

B. Salty. Season your plan with humor.

C. Simple. Be simple and prayerful in answering the Five Key Questions.

Chapter 15
THE SIX-MONTH RULE

GP

At this important point in the planning process, some people feel like yelling, "Help! I can't let go!" Yes, you can. God gave you the ability to do anything you really want to do—with His help. I learned that important fact from my parents when I was growing up. If I said, "But I can't," they invariably responded, "Patty, *can't* never could do anything, but *you* can with the help of God. Don't ever give up." I always thought they just said that so I would try harder, but they were always right.

Yes, you can let go. You may look at something you haven't used in a while and think, "But I may need this someday." If you think you will need it *some*day, ask yourself when was the *last* day you used it. A principle that will help you in separating is called *The Six-Month Rule*. It says, "If I haven't used it in six months and don't plan to use it in the next six months, I need to give it to someone else."

The only exceptions to this rule are occasional, specialty-use, seasonal, and maternity (!) items. Perhaps the occasion or event just has not arisen to use it. You may have a special dress or a tux hanging in the closet. If it's still a good fit, if you still like the color and style, if you honestly would wear it, and if you won't go out and buy something new if the occasion arose, then by all means you are justified in keeping it. You may have skis which you haven't used in a few years, but you plan to go skiing again. So keep them.

For all other items, ask yourself, "Have I used this in the last six months?" If not, why? There is a reason you haven't used it, and chances are good that if you haven't used it in the previous six months, you won't use it in the next six months.

I organized a large home for Patrick and Judy, a couple with a very close family who all live in Miami. Their four children are all grown, married, and have several children of their own. They both have a great sense of humor, and we had a lot of fun working together. Their home wasn't messy, but they had many years of hidden, accumulated belongings which they no longer needed. We set aside two full weeks to organize the most important areas of their home. We worked very hard and long hours, and after many days of organizing the kitchen, closets, attic, and garage, we purged and gave away many things.

Interestingly, a common answer kept popping up as I asked the key questions: "Have you used this in the last six months?" and "Will you use it in the next six months?" Although they were getting rid of a lot, they found many things which they were "saving" for their grown children. These things were not keepsakes (which I discuss in Chapter 25, "Ten Common Questions"), but those wonderful, usable items that for some reason they weren't using. We agreed to implement The Six-Month Rule. Patrick and Judy obviously hadn't used these items in years, but would their children use them within six months? We set up temporary places in the garage and labeled sections along the wall with each sibling's name on bright pieces of paper. As we came across things Patrick and Judy believed they couldn't part with because they were sure one of the children would surely want them, we put these things in that person's spot. Near the end of the project, we called all the children and their families over and asked them to take everything they wanted, but only if they would truly use them. How much was left? Most of it. Who was hanging on to all those things? Not the grown children, but the parents.

Although it was hard for them to "let go," they prayed and asked God to help them. He did. They were willing to be changed and ended up giving away a small truckload of items.

When you get stuck in the process, pray and ask God to help you. Look to His Word, where He gives us life and encouragement. Ask Him to speak to you and to help you make decisions to let go. The end result is that you will be free of the excess weighing you down.

THE SIX-MONTH RULE

If I haven't used it in six months
and don't plan to use it
in the next six months,
I need to give it
to someone else.

Chapter 16
NEVER STOP SEPARATING

GP

*And God said, "Let there be an expanse
between the waters to separate water from
water." So God made the expanse and
separated the water under the expanse
from the water above it. And it was so. God
called the expanse "sky." And there was
evening, and there was morning—the
second day. (Genesis 1:6-8)*

God continues to separate throughout creation. That's a lesson for us as we emulate Him in creating order in our lives. Even after we separate the darkness out of our lives and we identify stuff that we need to get rid of and purge, the separation process continues. It never, never stops. One of the secrets to getting organized and staying organized is to never stop separating.

Separating requires a *willingness to change*, and change is an on-going process. Today may be the time to separate that item we were holding onto yesterday. If you are willing to *keep changing*, you will be able to *keep separating*. When you are willing to pray and ask God to show you what needs to be kept and purged, He is always faithful to direct your steps. I am constantly amazed at His timing, love, and grace for us. He knows how much we can bear at each moment in our lives.

Kate, a lady who lived in New Orleans, is a good example of someone willing to continue the process of separating and "letting go" of old things. She was going through a painful divorce when she enlisted my help in organizing her move. Her home was very messy, which reflected the turmoil inside of her. We separated many things to give and throw away, and we prepared everything else she owned for packing. My goal was to facilitate a smooth move and enable her to get organized easily in her new home, so I then packed her according to the plan of order we established.

When she unpacked, she was able to set up her new home on her own and keep it organized, which certainly encouraged her and helped her overcome her previously bruised self-esteem and personal humiliation. She called periodically just to share her excitement of continued purging. "Remember that box of_____. I threw it out today," she told me with excitement and renewed energy.

When Kate was preparing to move to California a year-and-a-half later, she once again enlisted my help. This time, however, she had become so free of the physical and emotional clutter previously weighing her down, that with big smiles and great joy, she was able to purge many more things that she had been clinging to. We had about one-third less to pack this time.

Remember: Just because we have made the decision at some point to keep something doesn't mean we always need to keep it. Sometimes, we haven't been emotionally ready to get rid of a particular item in the initial stages of organizing—or in any stage of maintaining order in our lives. It may have been overwhelming for us to make those decisions at that time.

Begin right now by training your mind to automatically think about what items you can purge almost daily. For example:

—When you are getting dressed, always look to the right, left, above, or below each piece of clothing you are going to wear. When you see these other items, ask yourself, "Should I give this away?" When you are pulling a file folder, look at the papers in front of and behind the paper you are going to use, and think about throwing some away.

—When you put on makeup in your newly organized bathroom, purge that old makeup which was too hard to throw away two weeks ago. There is a reason you are not using it today, and you probably won't use it tomorrow. Get rid of it and simplify your life.

—In your workshop, look around and honestly ask yourself if it is time to get rid of that lamp that has been sitting there for twelve years waiting to be fixed. I know, last month you said that now since you were organized, surely you would fix it. Face it. It is not a priority; especially since you are much more organized now, you are able to spend more time doing the fun things you never had the time for before.

To help you continue separating, implement the *In and Out Rule:* "When something comes in, a similar item must go out." As an example, when you buy a new pair of shoes, pick out a pair to give away or throw away. If you buy a new dress, give one away. The same goes for nearly everything. If you honestly look at your belongings and can't purge an item in a similar category, pick something close by. If you purchase a new shirt and truthfully wear all your shirts, then pick another item of clothing to give away. The idea is that every time you bring something into your home, something must also go out. This rule is another secret to staying organized.

Ask yourself this question, "Am I willing to change my clutter habits by developing new habits of constantly separating? Instead of 'hanging on,' am I willing to 'let go'?" If the answer is "yes," then you are well on your way to staying organized!

NEVER STOP SEPARATING

A. Be willing to change.
B. Develop a habit of separating.
C. Implement the "In and Out Rule."

Chapter 17
SHELVE THE SHOULD'S

GP

I wish I had a nickel for every time I heard a person say: "Someone told me I *should* assign this type of item in this particular place, but I don't like it there." This statement has been repeated to me hundreds of times from clients and in seminars. When it comes to organizing, *shelve those should's!* Forget about them. Those ideas you heard may be very good suggestions and work very well for some people, but they may not be what works best for you at this particular time. As you continue to assign your items to specific places, *pull some of the ideas you like off the shelf* and use them as they are appropriate for you.

Remember that in organizing, there is no right or wrong way to do it. (This may not apply to the other areas of our lives!) The only thing you "should" do in organizing is purge your life of all the things God shows you to get rid of. Listen carefully to Him. He customized you when He created you; He knows your habits better than you do; and He knows what will work best for you personally. *Pray and ask His help during every step,* including the assigning stage. He is always faithful to help you.

Of the many kitchens I have organized, one I especially enjoyed organizing was for Nick and Lisa, a doctor and his wife in Chicago. When Lisa first called me for help, she explained that their kitchen needed remodeling since they didn't have enough space, and so she hired me to organize and help design a new kitchen. I love to cook, and kitchens are one of my favorite areas in the home to organize, so I was particularly excited about helping her. I have also found that when a kitchen is organized, it tends to enhance the way a family operates because it is an important area that affects the entire family.

When I arrived, I was somewhat surprised to see how large her kitchen really was. It had generous storage space, including a pantry. Lisa was very easy to work with, and she was eager to implement The Genesis Principle, ready to purge every unnecessary item, and willing to try new ideas. We happily worked through the first three steps of separating, combining, and evaluating.

When we came to the assigning step, we customized her kitchen in the following way: The first questions I asked her were, "What is important to your husband in the kitchen?" and "What considerations should we make concerning your two little children?" Her husband had a routine in the mornings: He walked into the kitchen from one door, searched for a big, to-go cup, went directly to the coffeepot, fixed his coffee with milk and sugar, walked out the door into the garage, and drove off to work.

The highest priority item we assigned were the to-go cups for her husband's morning coffee. Normally, I would have combined them together with all the other to-go cups, but not in this case. Both Lisa and her husband are very tall. We selected a cabinet directly in the path of his normal routine, picked only the cups that her husband particularly liked to drink from, and assigned them at the top of the cabinet where they were very easy for him to reach. I have never before nor since assigned the most used coffee cups, the ones used daily, the high priority/high usage ones, on a top shelf, out of reach for most people. However, this spot was perfect for them.

Lisa thought for a minute, then she said, "We probably should move the coffeepot." When I asked her why, she responded with, "I heard that I should have it closer to the sink." I explained that the only thing we *should* do is what works best for her and her husband, so we left the coffeepot where it had always been since they both liked it there. We now assigned the sugar and some spoons to a cabinet next to the coffeepot. Her husband was delighted. He now could walk into the kitchen, know exactly where to grab one of his favorite mugs, pour his coffee, be out the door, and still be whistling.

Try and imagine the impact of these small, but very important, high priority decisions! Many of you also start your day with great frustration over little things. Look at how we first implemented the Four Steps in their order, and how they led us to be creative with Lisa and her husband's needs. We shelved the should's and started customizing this kitchen based on the most important issue—helping her husband get started off to a good morning, in a happy frame of mind, as he faced the many intense pressures of his day. What could be more important?

Next, we considered her children and selected a drawer low enough for them to reach their little plastic cups. Now they didn't have to climb up on the counter to get a cup.

All of Lisa's other high priority/high usage items were assigned to very high places in the cabinets, way above and out of reach for most other people, including this short organizer! In fact, I had to climb up on top of a stool to organize them. They were completely out of my reach. Keep in mind these were the things that she used all the time. She didn't like having to bend, so she put only the low priority/low usage items down low. For someone else, their same exact high priority items might be assigned to low places and their low priority to high places.

The end result when we were finished was especially exciting. Lisa had room left over! Some drawers and cabinets had room to spare, and a few shelves were practically empty. She realized now there was no need to go to the extra expense of remodeling, so she decided to simply paint the cabinets and use the money for other improvements in their home. Between the coffee mugs and the end result of saving thousands of dollars, I don't need to tell you how thrilled we made her husband!

One more note about shelving the should's: Nearly everyone I have worked with finds items in their piles of clutter that are things they "should have done already." That may happen to you. It doesn't do any good to lament and feel guilty about all of those things we should have taken care of before now, but didn't because we couldn't find them under the piles of clutter. Put those should's on the shelf as well, and keep going. Say to yourself, "Now I am doing what I am supposed to be doing in getting organized." If it is something you really need to address, make a special note and put it in a specific place where you can address it after you are through organizing.

Don't stop. Keep your momentum up, and keep going. You're getting there!

SHELVE THE SHOULD'S

A. Put the "I should" thoughts on the shelf.

B. Pull the "I like" ideas off the shelf.

C. Pray for the best ideas.

Chapter 18
Dump That "Valuable" Junk

GP

A s I help people separate and assign all the things in
their closets and garages, they sometimes look at
an item longingly and ask me, "Do I really have to throw
this away? What if I need it someday?" They instinctively
know the thing they hold in their hand is junk, but they
still want to hang on to it. God's Word has every answer
for our lives, including learning how to throw away seemingly valuable junk. Here are some principles to help you
make these crucial choices:

A. Make the decision. In the act of creation, God made
many beautiful and useful things. Later, however, He
made the decision to throw away most of the wonders He
had made. When God saw how man was corrupting the
world, His heart was filled with the pain of man's rebellion (Genesis 6:5-8). He caused The Great Flood to wash
away the face of the earth.

   It's the same with us! Most of the possessions we acquire have a specific purpose at the time we buy them.

Months or years later, our needs change, and even possessions that were good for us may no longer be necessary or appropriate for us to keep. And sometimes we make purchases out of a rebellious heart. We didn't need these things at all. They were just attempts to fill up the emptiness in our hearts, and nothing but God Himself can fill that hole.

Pray, and ask God to change your heart and give you the desire and the strength to throw things away. At the same time, pray for a discerning heart to know what things God would have you keep. Only He knows your future needs. Finally, thank Him for His help in your decision-making process.

B. Clutter Corrupts. Make no mistake. The junk in our homes and offices is symbolic of the internal junk that God desires to clean out of our minds, hearts, and emotions.

Clutter builds a wall between us and those who are close to us. Some of us miss out on the blessing of fellowship with others because of the embarrassment of a messy house. The clutter distracts us from our most important responsibilities and prevents us from getting and keeping our finances in order. Most importantly, clutter builds a wall between us and God, and prevents us from being in a place to receive God's best blessings.

Just as God saw the corruption of the earth, we need to see that clutter corrupts our sense of peace and joy. This insight motivates us to throw away the material possessions which clog our lives and hinder our relationships.

C. Simplify. The account of Noah inspires us to make our lives simple so we can be undistracted as we follow the Lord. Noah was focused on doing what God called him to do. Nothing else mattered. God directed Noah to keep only the minimum and leave the rest behind. The things he left may have seemed valuable to him before he boarded the Ark, but the minute he stepped on that boat, they would have been hindrances to God's will for his life. Like Noah, if we are willing to be purified by throwing and giving away unnecessary possessions, we will have fewer distractions which might keep us from following the path God has graciously chosen for us.

Often, our extra possessions are the very things that meet the needs of other Christians. If we want to truly function as a New Testament Church, we'll provide for one another's needs from our own possessions. Then Christians won't go into debt for things they need. In Acts 2:44-45, Luke wrote about the giving and sharing among Christians: "All the believers were together and had everything in common. Selling their possessions and goods, they gave to anyone as he had need."

Don't be afraid to throw away and give away. It will clean out your clogged spiritual and relational arteries so you can feel more alive. As you use your possessions to help others, be thankful to God for the opportunity to bless others. Most importantly, we should thank God for the chance to clean up our lives before passing our clutter to another generation.

DUMP THAT "VALUABLE" JUNK

A. Make the decision.

B. Remember that clutter corrupts.

C. Simplify, simplify, simplify.

Chapter 19
LABEL LOGICALLY, LEGIBLY, AND LARGELY

GP

I love Georgia. I was born in New York to a beautiful Southern mother and a handsome Italian father. My parents met during World War II when my Dad was stationed in Atlanta. They continued to write when he was shipped out to Japan. After his discharge from the Army, they married and moved to New York where my brother and I were born. In the North, my Mom was labeled "that Southern gal" with her strong "y'all" drawl. When I was two, my parents decided the South was calling, so we moved to Atlanta where my Dad was labeled a "Yankee" with his strong Northern accent.

My parents never complained that these labels hurt them, but I suspect that being labeled didn't help either of them adjust to their new environments. If I were to label myself, I guess I would have to be called a "Y'all Yankee," a term which no one would understand without an explanation. Labels can help, confuse, or distract.

Labels are important when it comes to organizing. Before most of us get organized, we can find some of our things if we spend enough time digging through our stacks and piles, but no one else could possibly find them. As we get organized, we need to make sure everything is easy to find—by all those who might be looking. But they won't know if we don't tell them. Let your labels do the telling. Label all the plastic containers you use, and in some cases, the drawers and cabinets, too.

Labels save time and eliminate confusion. Just be sure the label is *logical* to others who may think differently from you. Remember that we are often not around when others may be looking for a particular item, and even if we are, we may not want to be interrupted. Be logical so that anyone, anytime can easily find what they are looking for.

Make sure anyone can read your label. Write clearly and make the letters *legible* and *large* enough so that everyone can read it. You may want to type labels on the computer or use a label maker, or you can hand-print labels using a permanent ink, felt-tip pen. Think about emergency situations. If you had to leave suddenly for a family emergency, or if something happened to you personally, are important items labeled logically and clearly enough to be found by someone trying to help you? If not, the confusion and delay could hinder their efforts to help because they don't have access to correct information. The same logic applies if you have to leave town suddenly and need someone else to send you important goods or papers. Be sure they can find them easily and quickly.

And proper labeling can also prevent other disasters. You may know that the reused spray bottle on the shelf contains ant poison, but someone else may think it's cleanser, like the original label says.

Labels come in many shapes, sizes, and colors. No matter what we are labeling, unclear labels cause confusion and loss of time or business. I was reminded of this recently when I discovered a cute, little restaurant located just outside a town on one of my well-traveled routes. I happened to stop next door and noticed tables and chairs inside, but I saw no sign in the window. Thinking it was a newly opened cafe, I went in just to look at their menu for future reference. I quizzed the lady who was standing behind the counter and appeared to own the shop, "How long have you been open?"

"Fourteen years," she responded.

I was stunned. I asked her, "Is there was a sign out front?"

"Oh yes," she responded.

"I guess I must have missed it," I told her. "Did you put it up recently?"

"No, it's been there fourteen years."

I silently wondered if I was beginning to lose my mind. I quickly looked at the variety of pizza, subs, and salads on the menu, then I made my way out the door. Once outside, I looked around for a sign. Nothing. Then I looked up. Sure enough, there was a very small sign on top of the building. It had one word: "Pizza." Even if I had seen the sign (and I hadn't, even though I had passed by dozens of times before), it didn't describe what the restaurant really offered. I like pizza at night, but my usual preference for lunch, especially while traveling, is something quick and light like a salad. I thought about the many times I had passed by, hungry for a salad but not pizza and had kept going, never knowing that a restaurant with a wide range on the menu was located in that building. I wish she had labeled her restaurant with a large, logical sign that gave accurate information. (It would also attract much more business.)

Whatever you are labeling, keep other people in mind, especially if certain things are commonly used by others in your household or office. Proper labeling will save time, eliminate confusion, and spare all of you a lot of aggravation and irritation.

BE SURE TO LABEL:

A. Logically
B. Legibly
C. Largely

Chapter 20
HELP! I'M OVERWHELMED!

GP

I t happens to the best of us. In the middle of organizing, we become uptight, overwhelmed, and anxious, and we don't know how to fix the situation. We don't know where to put things, and in our frustration and confusion, we think about all the other responsibilities which we have put on hold while we are organizing. The more stuff we pull out to separate, the more we realize we still have to do. The decision-making process sometimes is exhausting, and we feel like giving up. We think we'll never finish, and we wonder why we ever thought we could get our lives in order in the first place. We feel helpless.

Sound familiar? Take heart. Stop and take a big, deep breath. Go outside and get some fresh air. Focus on God. Listen to Him. Soak up His peace and understanding. He is the God of order, and He knows how you feel. He sees everything you own, He knows what you are going to need and when you'll need it, and He wants to help you. He is the God of the process as well as the finished product, and He delights in the progress you are making.

Organizing is the same as any project God calls us to do which is not within our normal skills, motivations, and strength. Recently, the Lord taught me a valuable lesson while I was retreating alone in a little house out in the country. Each morning, I rose early and sat on the back deck facing directly into the beautiful sunrise so I could experience that soothing comfort of the early morning sun on my face. With my eyes closed in the presence of God, I listened to the Lord and prayed for all the people and situations He brought to my mind. Those couple of hours each morning were wonderful, and I didn't want any morning to end. I soaked in every aspect of that time together—the fresh coolness of the morning air against my cheeks, the warmth of the sun against my eyes, the singing of the many birds all around me, and the sounds of little creatures bustling here and there in the bushes and trees.

Then I took a long walk, and I continued to pray. Later, I came back to begin working on the computer. Not only did I enjoy that time with the Lord together first thing in the morning, but it always brought me peace for the day and removed all anxiety about the many (it felt like millions!) things waiting for me to do back at the office and at home. Beginning each morning this way made each day flow much more smoothly.

One morning, however, just as I was waking up, I heard the Lord tell me to get on the computer first, before our wonderful quiet time together. This direction didn't make sense to me, but sometimes the Lord tells us to do things which don't make sense at the time. Very often while I'm organizing, the Holy Spirit directs me in a way that seems illogical, but it always turns out to be the best way. So that morning, I obediently sat down at my computer (a bit annoyed, I might add, at missing out on our quiet sunrise time together).

Much to my dismay, I immediately ran into two significant difficulties with my computer, and I experienced overwhelming frustration. Since I am not that savvy with computers, I usually call one of my faithful, obliging friends for help, but it was too early—and besides, I was out in the country without a regular phone. I was upset. *Very* upset. I felt helpless and prayed, "Lord, I thought You said to start here this morning, but all I'm running into are problems!" Within only a few minutes, solutions came to mind, and I discovered how to correct both problems easily. I sat amazed.

Just as suddenly, the peace of God engulfed me, and I heard Him speak to me about relying on Him to take care of all my needs, cares, concerns, and problems. He would teach me what to do and how to take care of each situation. If I understood that He is wise and that He cares, I wouldn't be overwhelmed. I needed to trust Him, relax, and follow His guidance step by step.

That's the way it is with organizing. God has all the answers, and He certainly knows how to help you. One of His purposes is that the organizing process will draw the two of you closer. As He reveals your inner clutter, you'll be more focused on truth and healing.

When you get frustrated, allow God to renew in your mind a picture of the finished, organized room, and how good you are going to feel when it is completely finished. I have found it very helpful to *meditate* on God's Word, *memorize* particular passages of Scripture, and *say* them out loud for encouragement while I'm organizing.

Studies have shown that when our ears hear our mouths verbalize something, our minds believe it all the more. That's why it is so important to be careful of the things we say to others and to ourselves.

Pray these scriptural prayers. Make them personal by inserting the word "me" in this way:

1. "The Lord bless me and keep me; the Lord make his face shine upon me and be gracious to me; the Lord turn his face toward me and give me peace." (Numbers 6:24-26)
2. "What is impossible with me is possible with You, God." (Luke 18:27)
3. "I can do everything through You, Lord, who gives me strength." (Philippians 4:13)
4. "I'm going to cast all my anxiety on You because You care for me." (1 Peter 5:7)

And believe it. He cares for you. Keep going, and allow our Creator to shower you with His overflowing kindness and graciousness, tender love, endless mercy, and a peace greater than any peace we could ever begin to understand or imagine. His peace will overcome that feeling of being overwhelmed. Nothing is too great nor overwhelming for our God.

WHEN YOU ARE OVERWHELMED:

A. Meditate on Scripture.

B. Memorize Scripture.

C. Say Scripture out loud.

Chapter 21
DON'T PUT IT OFF ANY LONGER

GP

Some people look forward to getting organized with the same joy as a person who is standing in the middle of a swarm of wasps. If these people are married, in desperation their spouses may have hired a Professional Organizer. They hope that a professional will get the ball rolling—finally.

If you are procrastinating with the excuse of being too busy, then you probably have a fear of getting organized much like the fear of getting stung by a wasp. Most people who get organized have busy lives, and that's why they are disorganized in the first place. The ones who have plenty of time are the ones who usually, but certainly not always, stay organized.

When people avoid dealing with their clutter, they are often afraid of what they might find—and especially, what they might find out about themselves. You may be one of those people. Be encouraged! The process is hard work, and sometimes we discover things that we have hidden for years, but I've never seen anyone "stung" by organizing. Ultimately, it can be an incredibly healing experience. So . . . don't run and hide.

Fear blocks our experience of receiving blessings from God. Fear may be very real, but it can be overcome. Mickey Wilson is a precious, petite lady in my church who never ceases to amaze me. This little 80 year-old, five-foot dynamo has more energy than most people half her age, and she has the faith to move mountains. She is a powerful prayer warrior. She is also a walking encyclopedia of natural health and herbs. I often call her for advice because she is the most up-to-date person I know on the topic of natural health. Her recommendations have usually proved to be right, so I listen carefully to her.

Mickey's experiences with wasps, bees, and other stinging insects are very unusual. Wasps, she explains, "smell" fear and attack a fearful person. The solution is obvious, she continues: We should not be afraid of them. Mickey never swings at wasps or bees, or tries to kill them. Instead, when a wasp buzzes around her, she stands still and takes authority over it. In the first chapter of Genesis, God told Adam to have dominion over all the animals in the world. Mickey takes that directive to heart, and she takes dominion over the wasps. She tells the wasp to come and rest on her finger, then she proceeds to escort the little creature away to the woods. As it flies off, she instructs it to stay away.

I know this story sounds strange, but I've seen her do this with my own eyes, or I wouldn't believe it. I've tried it, but I readily admit that I am still afraid even though I tell myself not to be. I am still more comfortable doing the normal thing: When I'm inside, I use a fly swatter, and when I'm outside, I hope and pray it'll go away! When I look at Mickey and her lack of fear, I learn some valuable lessons that we can apply if we procrastinate about getting organized.

First of all, if you are procrastinating, *stop using excuses.* Be honest. Admit that you may be afraid of what you may uncover about your things or about yourself. Admit that you may be protecting yourself with those walls of clutter surrounding you. The clutter may be embarrassing and frustrating, but it also gives you a measure of comfort. The clutter has been a part of your life for so long that it has become "normal" for you, and besides, there is so much of it that it may seem hopeless to even try to get organized. But remember: Change can heal, and order will strengthen you and your relationship with God as the confusion of clutter and disorder are removed.

Second, *take authority over your clutter.* You are more important to God than all the belongings you have. Moving those things out of the way will break down barriers in your relationship with Him. He will be delighted with the steps of progress and with the results—and so will you.

Don't think the clutter will just go away. It won't. You must take positive action.

Third, *don't run and hide. Nothing is impossible.* Your disorder isn't an impossible task to conquer. With the principles and examples in this book, you now have the simple tools to enable you to succeed.

God will help you through the difficult and seemingly insurmountable mountains of disorder. Meditate on this passage:

> *So do not fear, for I am with you; do not be dismayed, for I am your God. I will strengthen you and help you; I will uphold you with my righteous right hand. For I am the Lord, your God, who takes hold of your right hand and says to you, Do not fear; I will help you. (Isaiah 41:10,13)*

As the Chinese philosopher said, "The longest journey begins with a single step." Take that step today and begin the process of getting organized!

Don't Put It Off Any Longer

A. Stop using excuses.

B. Take authority over your clutter.

C. Don't run and hide. Nothing is impossible.

Chapter 22
HANDLES OF HOPE

GP

I have worked with all kinds of people—young and old; married and single; adults and children; men and women; professional and non-professional; black, white, and yellow; those green with envy and ones content with little; sad and happy; people who are hopeful and those who feel hopeless.

I have found a common denominator among all shapes, sizes, and types of people. The ones with a *sense of humor* are also the most *hopeful* about getting organized. People without a sense of humor tend to feel hopeless about their clutter. The hopeful have the ability to laugh at themselves and their situation, but the hopeless constantly criticize themselves. The hopeful laugh *with* one another; the hopeless laugh *at* others.

If a spouse or family member is critical of the disorganized person, that person often feels hopeless. In stark contrast, when the family member is understanding and loving, the one who is disorganized usually feels hopeful about his ability to get organized. The hopeful may feel frustrated at times, but he has courage to work through the problem. A hopeless person, however, thinks he is a lost cause. He feels he will always be stuck and helpless in his cluttered home and heart.

No matter how dark the situation, you can always find hope in God and in the truths of His Word. Thank Him for your weakness of disorder because it is an opportunity for Him to display His power, wisdom, and love in your life. I am a living example of my greatest weakness becoming my strength through the power of God working in my life. (If you haven't read it yet, see Chapter 2, "A Former Cluttered Mess.") I find renewed hope by meditating on Psalm 42:11, "Why are you downcast, O my soul? Why so disturbed within me? Put your hope in God, for I will yet praise him, my Savior and my God."

Many of my clients have expressed their initial fear of being the "impossible case"—my first "failure"—the "only one" who couldn't get organized. They feared they were "the worst" of all the people I've ever helped. "No," I assure them, "absolutely not." None of them were any of these things. I reassured them that everyone has the ability to get organized. It's just a matter of learning the principles for a life-style change. This change may be harder for some than others, and it will take a considerable amount of time and energy to get organized, but no one has failed yet when they were willing to make these changes.

Laugh! Find humor in your disorder. And if your spouse or family member is struggling with messiness, be that person's greatest cheerleader. Don't be critical of yourself or others; instead, be caring and kind. Humor is contagious and helpful. Proverbs 15:13 says, "A happy heart makes the face cheerful."

Sheryl, who works at my bank in Gainesville, Georgia, has a great sense of humor and is a good example of learning to laugh at our weaknesses. I've never met her in person, but when I called her on the phone for help with a problem on my checking account, she instantly found a way to laugh with me about being the organizer who has problems balancing those left-brained figures. She said that when she gets down about things, she thinks of her three favorite words: free, buffet, and clearance. Those words instantly explained her weaknesses! Her willingness to share them in a humorous way gave both of us a good laugh, which enabled me to laugh at myself and my own mistakes. Her lighthearted humor made my entire day better because it helped me feel better about myself. When I look at a picture of Jesus laughing which hangs in my church, I am often reminded of God's sense of humor. It always inspires me to look for "the lighter side" of things and laugh at myself even when I feel like crying. Proverbs 15:30 says, "A cheerful look brings joy to the heart, and good news gives health to the bones."

If you feel like crying when you look at the disorder around you, find something funny to laugh about. You may be surprised. Humor will give you strength to get started and keep moving. When you are tired, humor will help you get fired-up again. *Laughter is a gift from God.* Use it often, particularly when sorting through clutter, and you will find a renewed feeling of hope about organizing your life.

HANDLES OF HOPE

A. Humor is healing.
B. Humor is hopeful.
C. Humor is Heaven-sent.

Chapter 23
FINDING BALANCE

GP

B alance is an important part of getting organized. Some people are willing to take only a small step toward order, and they soon find themselves as messy as ever. Others, however, go too far and obsessively organize every closet, drawer, room, and person they can get their hands on. They want everything perfect, in its place, everywhere, all the time. ("Is that asking too much?" they ask.) Compulsively organizing can interfere with enjoying life, rest, and relaxation which God wants for us. Balance is one of God's great blessings to us. Just look at nature. Everything that God created is in perfect balance. What a great example right before our eyes! In the story of creation, we read:

> *And God said, "Let the land produce living creatures according to their kinds: livestock, creatures that move along the ground, and wild animals, each according to its kind." And it was so. (Genesis 1:24)*

Notice the similarity of the next verse:

> *God made the wild animals according to their kinds, the livestock according to their kinds, and all the creatures that move along the ground according to their kinds. And God saw that it was good. (Genesis 1:25)*

When God repeats Himself in His Word, He wants to emphasize something very important, and we need to pay close attention. All of the animals reproduced the same kind of animal. Nothing reproduced a different sort of animal or creature. Not then, not now, not over the centuries since then—not ever. From the very beginning and forever more, animals only reproduced their same kind. We would have a messy world if the animals were always reproducing something different. All of God's creation is precise and orderly. He made sure our home—the world—was in order and balanced before creating Adam from the dust of the ground. And if order is in balance in our lives, it will motivate those around us to find balance, too.

Having balance is a key to staying organized. If we spend a little (but not too much) time keeping things in order, it is easier to stay organized. We will have less frustration, and, needless to say, less conflict with our spouse, other family members, friends, and co-workers. Frustration and conflict are huge time-robbers. Without them, we'll have more time to devote to other things we enjoy.

To have this balance in our organizing, most of us need to change. If you are messy, you need to take the steps outlined in this book to get your home, your office, and your heart in order. And if you are the neat one in a marriage or office, you may need to change, too. For example, if your spouse is messy, you may be critical. You will need to change to be more affirming and supportive. Speak the truth, but in a way that makes it easier to hear. Paul wrote to the Colossians, "Let your conversation be always full of grace, seasoned with salt, so that you may know how to answer everyone" (Colossians 4:6). Don't blame; instead, encourage. As you allow God to change you, He may even use your affirmation and encouragement to begin to change those people around you.

Everyone can change and have balance, no matter how old they are. Look at Noah. He was 500 years-old before he had children (Genesis 5:32). I'm sure he had some adjustments to make after 500 years of ingrained habits.

If you are having difficulty with change, admit that you may be too set in your ways. Be willing to change. Ask for God's help, and take a step in the right direction. The more our habits are hardened, the more we need two things: God's grace and personal tenacity.

Raivis and Anna, an older couple in their late 60's, live in a quaint, but roomy older home on Long Island, New York. Both had been widowed, and of course, they had combined their two households. After nine years of marriage, they had accumulated even more things, but neither of them was willing to part with any of it. We worked in their basement, which was piled high with years and years of accumulated stuff. There was very little room to walk.

At first, I worked with Anna alone because I don't usually begin my work with couples together. (That can be disastrous.) As we sorted through each item, Anna kept saying, "That's Raivis'. He needs it and would never let us throw it out." Anna made this statement dozens of times. After a while, I realized we weren't making much progress at all. The mess was only shifting places.

In an attempt to break the logjam, I decided to work with Raivis alone. We went through the exact same pile of things, and he said, "That's Anna's. She needs it and would never let us throw it out."

In desperation, I decided to call their bluffs. I got together with both of them, and went through the same pile—now for the third time. Neither wanted to claim any ownership of the stuff, and neither was willing to admit being the one refusing to let go. I gently explained that since neither of them claimed allegiance to any of this stuff, it must have "just appeared" through the years. Certainly we could give or throw most of it away. In the next few hours, we barely made it through one small area of their basement, but somehow we filled a whole truckload of trash and a few bags of give-away. We made progress, but they couldn't finish the process. Within just a few weeks, the clutter from the rest of the basement made its way into the now-cleaned area, and it became a mess all over again. Both of them needed to change, but neither of them was willing.

Far too often, we want "the other person" to change, but we probably need to change ourselves. Be open and honest with God. Let Him show you how you need to change your attitude or actions in order to find balance in your own life, and to encourage others to find it in theirs. Ask God what He wants to change in you to bring balance into your home or business.

To Have Balance, We Must:

A. Be the one willing to change.

B. Agree to implement changes.

C. Be ready to keep on changing.

Chapter 24
HOW MUCH TIME?

$$\boxed{\text{GP}}$$

O n the fourth day of creation, God created the sun, moon, and stars to mark our seasons, days, and years. He brought order to our twenty-four hour days by giving us these signs to gauge our time. Perhaps God has appointed this season for you to bring order into your life. Just as God took time to order the world and the universe, it will take you some time to order your world.

> *And God said, "Let there be lights in the expanse of the sky to separate the day from the night, and let them serve as signs to mark seasons and days and years, and let them be lights in the expanse of the sky to give light on the earth." And it was so. God made two great lights—the greater light to govern the day and the lesser light to govern the night. He also made the stars. God set them in the expanse of the sky to*

give light on the earth, to govern the day
and the night, and to separate light from
darkness. And God saw that it was good.
And there was evening, and there was
morning—the fourth day. (Genesis 1:14-19)

God brought order to the light He created and created the very beginning of time as we know it. How much time does it take to organize? I have found that it typically takes *four to five times longer* to get organized than we think it will take. Does this surprise you? Does it discourage you? Realistic expectations are very important to help you plan appropriately and to give you the courage to stay motivated.

This principle is not a hard fast rule since everybody's belongings, clutter, and disorder are different, and each person works at different speeds. Some people make quick decisions, while others are slow, and interruptions dramatically cut into your time. But a general rule is to figure that if you think you can organize your closet in three hours, it will probably take you twelve to fifteen hours. If you think you can organize your bookshelves in one hour, you will probably need four to five hours.

Studies have shown that interruptions distract us for six minutes—in addition to the time of the actual interruption. As an example, let's say you are organizing your closet. You answer the phone and talk only ten minutes. You lose six minutes jotting down a note, thinking about what the person said, or getting distracted by something you see before you start organizing again. Including the ten minutes of conversation, you have actually lost sixteen minutes of productivity. If you have only two ten-minute phone calls in one hour, you would lose thirty-two minutes, or more than half of that hour! This principle is the same as driving on the expressway versus stop and go traffic. Every time you stop, it takes more time to get going again.

To organize correctly so that you stay organized, you will need to plan a considerable amount of time. If you have someone helping you, it will go much faster. Realistic expectations will give you assurance that you are doing a good job and accomplishing a lot. Remember that your disorder did not suddenly happen overnight. Neither will organization.

When I work with my clients, the amount of time I may spend on an average kitchen, closet, or office is often two full days, seven hours each day. As a Professional Organizer, I am totally focused on my client, and I push hard. I don't allow interruptions or distractions, and my client stays centered on making decisions the entire time. Every detail from start to finish is thoroughly organized. Two days of organizing a single room or closet is only a general example. I have spent much more time (even weeks!)—and occasionally less time—in different kitchens, closets, and offices with different people. One person working alone usually is slower, and it is easier for that person to get side-tracked. As a result, one person might need several more days to do the same job. Also, if the time is broken up among more days, you will have the loss of start-up time for each session.

Once a wife called to ask me if I would organize her home before her husband had surgery. They had a very large, two-story home and planned to put a hospital bed in the den on the first floor until he fully recovered. She called me a few days before his surgery and wanted me to come out the next day and organize her home. As always, I asked her many questions, including detailed descriptions of each room so I could get a mental picture of her home environment. She was very open and candid, as most of my clients are, as she described the piles of clutter and junk and papers everywhere. She said there was an extra bedroom with a single bed, but this bed was completely hidden by all the stuff piled on it and around it.

I wasn't surprised by her description of her home. I've organized many rooms just like it, but extremely cluttered rooms take more time to organize. As she described each room in her home, it sounded like each closet, room, and drawer were just as cluttered as that bedroom! She had four small children, and their toys were scattered all over the house. She admitted that she shopped a lot, and she never wanted to throw away anything. Clutter made her feel comfortable. The more she talked, I became increasingly aware that she wasn't committed to purging things from her cluttered home. She was only temporarily desperate to make things look neat and please her husband.

I didn't see her clutter as "the problem." But two challenges were apparent: First, she was unwilling to admit that she needed to get rid of a significant part of her stuff, and second, she had an unrealistic expectation of how long the process of organization would take. A lack of commitment to be ruthless with clutter always leads to indecision, and each decision then takes far more time to make.

Based on my analysis of her perspectives, I gently explained that in the day she had allotted, we could only organize her den, dining room, and hall to make it pleasant for her husband's recovery. Organizing her entire home, I told her, would take a strong commitment and hard work for several days each week for a few months.

Since my schedule was full at the time, I sent another organizer out to work with her. Occasionally, I worked with both of them as an advisor. At first, she was excited and enthusiastic and scheduled regular organizing days each week. She was making considerable progress, and we were greatly encouraged. However, she soon realized that getting organized meant getting rid of two-thirds of all of the piles of junk, and that it always took more time than she planned. Several months later, her house was still not completely finished. She slacked off because it became increasingly difficult for her to part with the security of her clutter. You can well imagine the stress and tension that this very large and very messy home created in her relationship with her husband and children. If she had been consistently willing to let go, and if she had invested as much time into organizing as she did into shopping, she could have most assuredly had a beautiful and enjoyable home by the end of the year.

You can have a beautiful home or professional office by setting realistic goals for yourself and the rest of your household or office. Allow the proper amount of time, and you will stay motivated and on course. Don't stop—keep the process going no matter how much stuff you have to wade through. Set your path straight, and stay on course no matter how much time it takes. Organizing your home or office will take time, so make up your mind to stay with the task until you are finished. Do you remember the old story of the tortoise and the hare? The winner of the race was the one who plodded on and didn't quit, not the one who started fast.

To help you stay motivated, take "before" and "after" pictures. They will show you how much progress you are making.

Don't quit. You're getting there!

How Much Time Does It Take To Get Organized?

A. It usually takes four to five times longer than expected.

B. Each interruption costs six extra minutes.

C. Set realistic expectations, and plan appropriately.

Chapter 25
TEN COMMON QUESTIONS

GP

My clients and those who attend my seminars are just like you: They want help with their mess. Their stories are varied, but they ask many of the same questions. For that reason, I want to include this chapter on the ten questions I am asked most often.

1. "Do I have to throw away my keepsakes?"

No, of course not. Keepsakes are very important. Use the Genesis Principle Four Steps with your keepsakes: A. *Separate* the keepsakes from the rest of your belongings. Purge the ones with unpleasant memories. Make sure the only ones you keep are the ones with good memories attached, the ones that put a smile on your face and make your heart sing. (This principle obviously does not apply to keepsakes from deceased loved ones. These may make you cry. If your tears are from missing them, that is normal, and you should keep those items and cherish those memories. But if you look at a keepsake and it stirs up bad memories about your relationship with them, or reminds you of any sin, first ask God to forgive you for any anger, bitterness, or other sin, and then get rid of those things.)

B. *Combine* them with other keepsakes.

C. *Evaluate* which ones you might access more often.

D. *Assign* a place for them in a plastic box or chest. Depending on your need and storage place, different sizes of plastic boxes, including under-the-bed boxes, work great. Get separate boxes for different members of your family. Put labels on the outside showing what and whose they are.

2. "I admit that I am still struggling with letting go. How can I take that step of throwing and giving things away?"

Adopt the "Caretaker Principle" which helps us draw back and say, "We are not owners, but caretakers." Everything belongs to God. He has just loaned us all the things in our possession. If we are not fully using certain items, then we are not "taking the proper and designated care" of them. Therefore, it's time to give them to someone else to "take care of them."

Find a good charity and give them lots of your things. Keep in mind that your excess and unused items may be answers to the prayers of others. What a blessing to take the things that clutter our spaces and give to people who really need them! If you are afraid to give something away because you may need it later, trust God to supply all your needs. In the past ten years of organizing, I can honestly say that I've only heard two people ever tell me they needed something they had given away.

A heart-warming example of someone implementing the "Caretaker Principle" is the story of nine-year old Sarah, the daughter of my friends, Beth and Mark. Beth had been sharing with her family all the principles she was learning about organizing. Without any prompting at all, Sarah decided to go through her clothes and take out all the ones she wasn't wearing. She piled them up and asked her Mom what to do with them. They prayed about it, and the next day at work, Beth heard about a family whose home had burned a few nights before. They had a daughter who needed the exact size clothing which Sarah had just purged from her closet! What a blessing to know that God led Sarah to share her clothes with someone in need before they even knew the need existed. Our God is a good God who knows our needs before we do.

Remember that we are not going to take anything with us when we go to be with the Lord, so let's not act like it. As a pastor put it one time, "I never saw a U-Haul trailer being pulled behind a hearse." The apostle Paul agreed with this pastor. He wrote:

> *But godliness with contentment is great gain. For we brought nothing into the world, and we can take nothing out of it. (1 Timothy 6:6-7)*

3. "I would like to have a heart change about my belongings so that I am more free of the wants and desires of things. How can that happen?"

An activity that will touch your heart is to work with the homeless in your area. Most major cities have programs to minister to the poor and homeless. You can work whenever you are able, without a long-term commitment. Every time I do, I come home with an intense desire to get rid of more things. What a blessing to help the homeless! Try it. You'll be surprised at the wonderful people you will meet and how they will bless you. It is humbling. We have encouragement from the believers in the early church. Luke recorded:

> *All the believers were one in heart and mind. No one claimed that any of his possessions was his own, but they shared everything they had. With great power the apostles continued to testify to the resurrection of the Lord Jesus, and much grace was upon them all. There were no needy persons among them. For from time to time those who owned lands or houses sold them, brought the money from the sale, and put it at the apostles' feet, and it was distributed to anyone as he had need."*
> *(Acts 4:32-35)*

And John wrote:

> *If anyone has material possessions and*
> *sees his brother in need but has no pity on*
> *him, how can the love of God be in Him?*
> *Dear children, let us not love with words*
> *or tongue but with actions and in truth.*
> *(1 John 3:17-18)*

4. "What about all of my magazines? I have a lot of money invested in them."

No amount of money can substitute for the freedom you will experience when you get rid of magazines. Keep only two of each subscription. Use the "In and Out Rule." When one magazine comes in, one must go out.

People hold onto magazines because they fear missing out on some great piece of knowledge. Magazines give us all the wrong messages, especially women. They tell us we are too fat—right next to a picture of a luscious desert and an article describing how we need to become terrific cooks. Cancel all subscriptions except two of your favorites. If your magazines are piling up, then that is a clear sign they need to go. An exception would be reference magazines such as business or home gardening. In such cases, put them in magazine boxes or special baskets. Then when the containers holding them are full, you know that it is time to purge them again. Recycle them, if possible.

5. *"Should I have a garage sale?"*

Most of the time, no. The time, effort, and energy it takes to put on a garage sale is the same as organizing. It usually takes four to five times longer and is four to five times harder to put on a garage sale than anyone thinks or remembers. However, if you have plenty of extra time and a whole lot of energy, you may want to consider it. Make sure that if you have one, you and your household are all in agreement and you are disciplined enough to haul off everything leftover—yes, absolutely everything—to a charity the next day. Don't bring any items back into your house!

I recommend that you give your goods to ministries and individuals who can use them. You surely will be blessed if you do. Jesus related the blessings of giving to the unfortunate: "The King will reply, 'I tell you the truth, whatever you did for one of the least of these brothers of mine, you did for me'" (Matthew 25:40).

6. *"I love to shop, and I have a hard time buying only a few things. I always buy more than we need and spend more than I should. What can I do?"*

Stop shopping altogether. Seriously. Go on a "shopping fast." It will change your life for the better. Don't buy anything that is not an absolute necessity, like food and toilet paper, for 30 days. Then notice how well you survive during those 30 days. In one month, a shopper can bring home a minimum of 77 pounds of "stuff," and this month's stuff may well be next year's clutter. You will be surprised to realize you can live without a lot of things you thought were "necessities."

After the 30 days, when you have needs, pray and ask God to supply them before just automatically going out and buying them. If you feel a peace about going shopping, then ask the Lord to show you where to go. I am often amazed at how He will direct me to a particular store where I find the item I'm looking for is on sale. Have a list of what you need and commit to buying nothing more than what is on the list!

God is our Provider. He likes having that opportunity to provide for us if we will allow Him.

7. "Does TV have any effect on the clutter in my home?"

Yes, turn it off and leave it off. Television is hazardous to your spiritual and emotional health. Very little on television is wholesome or uplifting. Our children (and we) see killings, blood, rebellion, sex, and crime—many times depicted as "normal." Adults laugh at all the wrong jokes, and families no longer communicate.

If you must watch television, be very selective. Limit your family and yourself to no more than one hour a night. Spend time talking, reading, or playing family games. Commercials describe all the things you want to have, and they fool you into thinking you need to have them, which adds to more clutter. These ads breed discontent and disorder in your home. Take televisions out of your children's rooms because they often watch programs that young, impressionable minds should not be seeing. And it wastes their precious time.

8. *"Is disorder more prominent with men or women?"*

Neither. I have worked with as many men as women, and I've noticed that their order and disorder is more a matter of their personality and how they were created. Their habits were established as they grew up and at that time, they learned (or failed to learn) discipline. Additionally, progress in getting organized is based on how much desire, willingness, and discipline people have, not their gender. The biggest difference I have seen is that men's closets are full of hats, and women's closets are full of shoes.

9. *"What if I truly can't decide on what to do with something?"*

If you can't decide, put it aside. Come back to it when you have gone through other things. Usually, the answer will suddenly become clear to you. Remember to pray and ask God to help you in the decision process.

10. *"Are you absolutely sure these principles will work for me? I think I'm beyond all help."*

Yes, I am sure they will help you if you give them a fair try. No one is beyond help. I've seen it all, and God's Word works for us in every area of our lives. You just have to have a willing heart.

Chapter 26
THE FINISHING TOUCH

GP

On the sixth day of creation, we find a very important lesson in organizing. God took a good look at everything He had made: the light, the sky, and the dry ground; the vegetation, seed-bearing plants and trees; fruit and vegetables; the sun, moon, stars and 24-hour days; birds, fish, livestock, creatures, and wild animals; and finally, His creation of male and female in His own image. And He was pleased that it was complete.

> *God saw all that he had made, and it was very good. And there was evening, and there was morning—the sixth day. Thus the heavens and the earth were completed in all their vast array. (Genesis 1:31-2:1)*

Everything, all of creation, was put in order—the environment, man, and food for man. God's work of creating order in the world was very good, perfect, and complete. He was finished.

Look at your own creation of order in your life. Are you able to say that it is "very good"? Is it complete? While God's creation was perfect, ours won't be. And ours never will be perfect because we are fallible people who live in a fallen world. But the final step in organizing, and one of the secrets of staying organized, is to completely finish the process. A good test of whether or not you are finished is to stand back, look at your newly organized area and honestly ask yourself, "Is it very good?"

When I was first organizing in 1989, I noticed that some of my clients stayed organized, but others went right back to their messiness. For a long time, I couldn't figure out the secret of success for those who stayed organized. I finally began to see a pattern which, after organizing hundreds of clients, has held true to this day. Several factors are involved, but the single most important difference is that the ones who *finish* getting organized *stay* organized. The ones who only did one room in a house, or one part of a room, or the closet but not the rest of the bedroom, or only the desk and a few file drawers in an office but not all the file cabinets, ended up messy again— one hundred percent of the time. But those who finished everything stayed organized.

You will know your work of organizing is good and finished when that area has a certain new "sparkle" and radiance to it. It will shine with the light of order if all the darkness is purged, given away or thrown away. Ask God to show you when things are complete. It truly will take on a different look. When things are "just right" in any particular area, you'll feel good about it and be satisfied with it. Our homes and everything in them should reflect the pure love of our Lord. Psalm 34:5 says, "Those who look to Him are radiant; their faces are never covered with shame." In the same way, when the shame of our clutter and excess is gone, our homes become radiant with His presence.

A good example of this is the home I organized for Christopher and Terri, a lovely couple who live in Houston, Texas, with their two teenage sons, Tom and John. We worked in Terri's walk-in closet first. She gave away many of her clothes. We pulled the out-of-season clothes and stored them in the guest room closet, rearranged the shelves, and then hung all the similar clothes together on nice, new plastic hangers. When we were finished, we then stood back to view our great accomplishment. The closet appeared orderly and picture-perfect, yet as we both stood there looking at each section of the closet, something just didn't seem right. So we prayed. Immediately, Terri saw a few more things that could come out of the closet and be given away, and I saw something that needed to be rearranged. These final changes made it easier for Terri to dress in the mornings. We stood back again and now her closet had that special "sparkle," and we knew we were ready to move on to another area of the house. That was six years ago, and to this day, Terri's closet still sparkles with neatness and order.

Next, we worked on Christopher's home office and library which had many shelves full of personal books. The three of us purged books, then Terri and I organized according to categories. When we were through, all three of us surveyed the newly organized, neat shelves. Everything looked perfect, but once again, it seemed to lack that special radiance when things are completely purged. We prayed, and God began to show Christopher several more books that needed to go. Once they were removed, the shelves took on a new look. When I worked with their two boys in purging clothes, tapes, and books from their rooms, they, too, looked for that completed, radiant look before saying we were truly "finished." Needless to say, this family's entire home looked and felt quite different when our organizing project was completed. Later, they all remarked at how much more peaceful their house seemed.

Think of disorder like a germ. It spreads from the basement to the upstairs, or from the bedroom back into the closet, or from the kitchen back into the pantry. Disorder will contaminate the other areas with clutter. Clutter collects in corners and mysteriously expands. Once you start getting organized, you must make a commitment to keep the process going and completely finish. Even if you only have time to devote a few hours a day every week, stay with it. Don't stop and don't give up!

Chapter 27
REST AND ENJOY

GP

Incredible blessings are waiting for those people who choose to work through the organization process and put their lives in order. With the excess clutter gone and the ability to find most anything they need in thirty seconds, people often tell me about the peace and rest they experience. Homes and offices feel more peaceful and enjoyable. Lines of stress actually disappear from their faces. Once my life was organized, people started telling me I looked ten years younger. (Maybe I could get organized again and lose a few more years!)

One lady I know, Elizabeth, lives in Charlotte, North Carolina. She has encouraged many others with her enthusiasm and tenacity in organizing. She says organizing is "contagious." She jumped in with both feet and was determined to get her entire life in order. After attending several of my seminars and reading the materials and scriptures numerous times, Elizabeth owned and implemented the principles. Over a period of time, she was able to organize most of her home on her own, and then she tackled her office as well. She broke free from the bondage caused by her mess and her family's clutter.

One Sunday after church, another lady walked up to Elizabeth and asked her a startling question. "You have such a beautiful glow on your face. Are you by any chance pregnant?" This type of question can indeed be startling to a woman who has already had her family and not planning on any more children. Fortunately, Elizabeth has a wonderful sense of humor, so with a great big smile, she replied, "No, I have just finished organizing my office and most of my home. I feel so free and happy. Now I have much more time to spend with my family. I know that when I go into my office on Monday morning, I'll be able to find anything I need. That feeling relieves me of a great deal of stress." Although the other lady was a bit embarrassed, Elizabeth considered it a high compliment that the benefits of organization would show on her face.

When others have finished organizing, I've seen that glow on their faces too, including men—and none of them were pregnant! Order frees you to be the person God created you to be. It frees you to rest when you need it, and to be able to enjoy life.

The seventh day of creation was designed especially for this purpose of rest:

> *By the seventh day God had finished the work he had been doing; so on the seventh day he rested from all his work. And God blessed the seventh day and made it*

holy, because on it he rested from all the work of creating that he had done. (Genesis 2:2-3)

Our seventh day should be set aside for worship of our Creator, rest, relaxation, and fun. God rested, not because He was weary, but because He was finished with His work and wanted to stop and celebrate it.

Although our work on this earth is never finished, and there is always something to be done, we can celebrate our Creator and the blessings He has given us. Most of my clients initially reported that they worked almost every Sunday but still felt behind. There never seemed to be a time when they felt like they were caught up. The harder they worked, the more behind they felt.

Working seven days a week is not healthy mentally, emotionally, spiritually, or physically. You will suffer, and if you have a family, they too will suffer. Worst of all, your relationship with God will suffer.

When I organize clients, I usually focus first on putting their physical environment in order, and then organize their time. Once the physical surroundings are organized, they naturally have more time and it is much easier to see the areas where they need to prioritize their time. However, one of my first recommendations is to take Sundays off (or Saturday, for my Jewish friends).

In the previous chapters of learning to organize, we have been emulating the steps God took as He created order in the world. Don't neglect this last step. The God of all creation saw the need for a day of rest, and He was setting an example for us. Certainly we should follow His steps. The Lord told Moses and the people to follow His example, "Six days you shall labor, but on the seventh day you shall rest" (Exodus 34:21). A day of rest means no shopping, cutting of grass, cleaning house, working at the office, and no organizing. How freeing to know you are not going to have to do any work on that day! Except for emergencies and unusual circumstances, develop the habit of putting everything else aside. If you stop shopping on Sundays, you will help other people take that day off. Many business studies have shown that when people take selected time off each week, they are much more healthy, alert, productive, and less accident prone for the rest of the work week. You deserve that wonderful day of rest, and getting organized will help it to be more relaxing and enjoyable.

As you tackle your organizing, remember that the One who first established order will be there to help you through every step. God is in the business of taking on seemingly impossible organizing situations. Nothing is too hard for Him, and none of us is beyond His help. Just look at His track record of organization, such as the huge Exodus Project. God gave Moses an incredibly challenging job of keeping order while he led two million rebellious Israelites across the desert to freedom. Moses was overwhelmed, exhausted, and sometimes he didn't know what to do nor where he was going. But he had confidence in God. Moses cried out to God for assurance. "The

Lord replied, 'My Presence will go with you, and I will give you rest' " (Exodus 33:14).

In God's presence we find rest physically, mentally, emotionally, and spiritually. When you are working on your organizing projects, God will be with you. He knows how to help you with every detail. If you will just ask Him, He will come.

Do you have a personal relationship with God our Father and the Lord Jesus Christ as your Savior? If not, stop and take the time right this minute to invite Jesus into your heart. There is no better time. Simply ask Him to reside within you.

God loves you so much that He gave His only Son, Jesus, so that anyone who believes in Him shall not perish but have eternal life. To everyone who receives Him, He gives the right to become children of God. Repent of your sins and believe in the Lord Jesus, and you will be saved. We are all sinners. Ask Him to forgive you, then confess with your mouth, "Jesus is Lord" and believe in your heart that God raised Him from the dead. Everyone who calls on the Name of the Lord will be saved.

If you would you like to receive Jesus now, pray this prayer:

> Dear Lord Jesus, thank you for your love for me. I admit that I am a sinner, and I ask for your forgiveness. I know that no matter how good I am, I cannot save

myself from Hell. I believe that God the Father raised you from the dead, and eternal life is mine if I believe in you. I now ask you to come into my heart and be Lord of my life. Thank you. Amen.

If you prayed that prayer (or your own prayer of faith in God's forgiving grace), you can be assured of His forgiveness and love because He promised to make you His beloved child. Pick up a Bible and begin reading in the Gospel of John. As you begin each chapter, ask God to give you fresh insight and faith in His love, forgiveness, and power. And feel His loving presence fill the inner closets of your life.

Many people initially pick up this book because they are discouraged about the clutter in their lives. Don't give up! If God can help me, He can certainly help you! He will give you direction and hope as you take steps to organize your life.

About the Author

Patty Chirico is the founder and owner of Jericho Enterprises, which was begun in 1989. Patty teaches people to apply Biblical principles of organization to our messy lives. When we become free of the clutter that weighs us down, we are then able to meet our goals and become all that God intends for us. A former cluttered mess herself, Patty understands the embarrassment, shame, and low self-esteem attached to our walls of clutter. After years of hiding behind mountains of paperwork and disorder, Patty discovered basic principles of order that began to transform her life in powerful ways.

Patty's services range from speaking and conducting seminars and retreats for businesses, churches, and professional organizations to working with individuals in their offices and homes. She is humorous, entertaining, dedicated, and motivating as she applies Biblical truths to modern lives.

The basic principles of "Organizing Our Lives" have been featured on numerous television and radio talk shows, including Larry Burkett's international radio program, "How to Manage Your Money," with Christian Financial Concepts. She has taught organizational skills at Georgia State University and in seminars across the United States and Europe.

Patty was privileged to become one of the first Professional Organizers to speak on the subject in Holland, and therefore, was instrumental in pioneering Professional Organizing in Europe. She is a member of the National Association of Professional Organizers (NAPO) and the Georgia Association of Professional Organizers.

For More Information

I f you would like information about scheduling Patty for speaking, organizing, consulting services, or to order more books, please feel free to contact her at:

Jericho Enterprises, Inc.
Box 177, 130-C John Morrow Pkwy.
Gainesville, GA 30501 USA
Telephone: 770.535.4557
E-mail: pchirico@trusted.net

Visit our web site at:
www.jerichoenterprises.com

Do you have a great organizing idea which you have used and which works? We welcome your ideas, comments, and suggestions. Other books, videos, and tapes are on the drawing board in the "Organize Your Life" series, and we may be able to use your idea. If you are the first to submit your suggestion and we use it any of our publications, we may be able to include your name.

However, we can't guarantee the use of your name because many people have similar ideas, and often they are duplicates of concepts we are already using in our work. All submissions become the property of Jericho Enterprises, Inc.

NEED HELP WITH ORGANIZING YOUR FINANCES?

Most of Patty's clients who struggle with clutter are also struggling to put their finances in order. For help, we highly recommend Christian Financial Concepts. They are a ministry committed to teaching Biblical principles of finances and managing money. You can contact them at:

Christian Financial Concepts
601 Broad St. SE
Gainesville, GA 30501
1.800.722.1976
770.534.1000

Or visit their web site at:
www.cfcministry.org